LINKEDIN
MADE
SIMPLE

FAT STRATEGIES IN A THIN BOOK

RYAN RHOTEN & ANDY FOOTE

Table of Contents

Part 1: Connect

Part 2: Converse

Part 3: Convert

Acknowledgments

Ryan here. I think Isaac Newton's famous statement best sums up the acknowledgment section of every book: "If I have seen further, it is by standing on the shoulders of giants." This statement could not be more accurate for me when it comes to LinkedIn.

Maybe like yourself, I've used LinkedIn since the beginning, which is to say I created a profile. At first, it was exciting. Then it was boring. Then I was like, WTF? But through the wisdom and guidance of many people (giants), LinkedIn has become not only exciting but essential. Today, LinkedIn is my go-to platform, and I think by the end of this book, it will be yours too.

The LinkedIn light bulb started to shine for me after an interview on my podcast with LinkedIn giants Jane Anderson and Kylie Chown, who co-authored the book *Connect*. During that interview, they helped me begin to see the power of LinkedIn by using it for only seven minutes a day.

Like a dimmer switch moving up towards its highest setting, LinkedIn giant David J.P. Fisher, who wrote the foreword for this book, moved the switch a little higher after we chatted about his first book, *Networking in the 21st Century*. During this discussion, he talked about the importance of using LinkedIn as a networking tool, a concept he expanded on in his latest book *Hyper-Connected Selling*.

Interviews with other LinkedIn giants such as Gina Riley, Mark Anthony Dyson, Sarah Johnston, Mary Henderson, Adrienne Tom, AJ Wilcox, Warwick A. Brown, Marc Miller, Jane Jackson, Don Orlando, Richard Kirby, Hannah Morgan, and many others continued to push the switch higher.

When I discovered Andy Foote, the switch moved to the brightest setting. Unlike myself, Andy saw the value of LinkedIn from the start. He has not only used LinkedIn to build his business and extensive network, but he uses it in service to others as well. Andy is always there with "the perfect tip" that turns the light on for so many others.

Andy is a genuine LinkedIn giant, and I'm honored to have co-written this book with him; a book, by the way, that is packed with so many strategies it should be twice the size. But, honestly, I'm glad it's not twice the size because maybe, just maybe, my children might read it.

*   *   *

My turn. When Ryan suggested we combine forces and write a book together, I didn't hesitate. Ever since he interviewed me on his podcast, *The BRAND New You Show*, I've been keeping tabs and taking notes. Ryan is a doer, and he knows his stuff; he's also an incredibly generous and genuine human being. I asked him about adding an audiogram to my podcast last year. He sent me two videos walking through how he did it. Two videos! Who does that? Ryan Rhoten does.

Over the years, many people have regularly suggested that I write a book to share my LinkedIn knowledge. One of the reasons I resisted was the concern that anything I wrote would eventually become incomplete or incorrect because LinkedIn is always changing and evolving. To minimize this, I've focused on core areas and techniques, which I hope will remain "evergreen."

One of the best things for me about working in LinkedIn coaching and writing about LinkedIn is that you're never alone and always have great colleagues to learn from and engage with. Although some of us have different approaches and utilize different strategies, there's a tremendous esprit de corps, which comes from a shared purpose and unbridled enthusiasm for our favorite platform. It's true: birds of a feather flock together.

In addition to the great people listed above, I'd add Richard van der Blom, John Espirian, Mark Williams, Alexander Low, Mic Adam, Liam Darmody, Joel Lalgee, Austin Belcak, Ariel Lee, Cher Jones, Kate Paine, Lea Turner, Mary Henderson, Judi Fox, Krista Mollion, and Madeline Mann, to name a few.

Thanks for suggesting we write this book together, Ryan. It's been a highlight of my career, and I think it will help many people.

Links and Profiles Mentioned

PROFILES

- Gina Riley - https://w.linkedin.com/in/ginariley/
- MarkAnthony Dyson - https://www.linkedin.com/in/markanthonydyson/
- Sarah Johnston - https://www.linkedin.com/in/sarahdjohnston/
- Mary Henderson - https://www.linkedin.com/in/maryhendersoncoaching/
- Adrienne Tom - https://www.linkedin.com/in/adriennetom/
- AJ Wilcox - https://www.linkedin.com/in/wilcoxaj/
- Warwick Brown - https://www.linkedin.com/in/warwickabrown/
- Marc Miller - https://www.linkedin.com/in/mrmiller/

- Jane Jackson - https://www.linkedin.com/in/janejackson/
- Don Orlando - https://www.linkedin.com/in/donorlandocareercoach/
- Richard Kirby - https://www.linkedin.com/in/richardkirbyatl/
- Hannah Morgan - https://www.linkedin.com/in/hannahmorgan/
- Richard van der Blom - https://www.linkedin.com/in/richardvanderblom/
- John Espirian - https://www.linkedin.com/in/johnespirian/
- Mark Williams - https://www.linkedin.com/in/mrlinkedin/
- Alexander Low - https://w.linkedin.com/in/alexanderlow/
- Mic Adam - https://www.linkedin.com/in/micadam/
- Liam Darmody - https://www.linkedin.com/in/iamliamd/
- Joel Lalgee - https://www.linkedin.com/in/recruitmentmarketing1/
- Austin Belcak - https://www.linkedin.com/in/abelcak/
- Ariel Lee - https://www.linkedin.com/in/edjariellee/
- Cher Jones - https://www.linkedin.com/in/itscherjones/
- Kate Paine - https://www.linkedin.com/in/katepaine/
- Lea Turner - https://www.linkedin.com/in/lea-turner/
- Judi Fox - https://www.linkedin.com/in/judiwfox/
- Krista Mollion - https://www.linkedin.com/in/kristamollion/
- Madeline Mann - https://www.linkedin.com/in/madelinemann/

Foreword

When the pandemic and its attendant social distancing hit in 2020, everybody and their mom suddenly called themselves a LinkedIn expert. That's because the trend towards digital business accelerated overnight. Tools like LinkedIn have been around for over a decade, but now people have had to use them. If you can't network in person—heck, if you can't even meet in person—virtual engagement becomes really important.

Lots of people wanted to cash in on that. But it takes more than a few LinkedIn posts and a five-page eBook to be a LinkedIn expert (shhh, don't tell all the gurus out there...you'll make them cry). That's why you are lucky you're starting in with *LinkedIn Made Simple*. This isn't a fluffy book of answers you could find with a thirty-second Google search. This is a fully mapped-out approach to social networking that will get results.

Here's why I think you'll get a lot out of this book if you apply its lessons: Because I like and trust Ryan and Andy. And this isn't a popularity contest thing. I have a best-selling LinkedIn book of my own under my belt, so I don't have to kiss up to anyone. But there's a concise list of fellow LinkedIn experts that I go to when I have questions, want feedback, or want to see what direction that site is going. Ryan and Andy are both on that list. If either of them wrote a book, I'd tell people to check it out. But both of them working together? It'd be foolhardy not to read it.

Because what they both understand, and what you will learn as you go through the book, is that LinkedIn is simply a tool. But a potent tool. It's a force multiplier, just like a lever or a pulley. It allows you to engage in business conversations and relationships in a way and at a scale that we just couldn't before. They'll show you how to do that for your professional life. But even though it's simple, they also know it's not easy. It takes work. And they don't subscribe to the shortcuts and hacks that are ubiquitous on LinkedIn.

These guys want you to be successful, and they aren't going to sell you snake oil or miracle tonics. They will show you a blueprint that will allow you to move your career forward using LinkedIn. So here's my suggestion: Read the book straight through as fast as you can. As they say on the cover, it's a thin book. But that's just to get the flavor and to give you the 50,000-foot view. Then, start from the beginning again, and step-by-step, do what they tell you to.

Do the messaging homework, sit at your desk, map out the story you want to share, and figure out your audience. Make your profile resonate with your target audience (and take the time to understand who that audience is), then create a network and engage with those people. Have conversations, share ideas, ask questions, and participate.

You'll find soon enough that you are getting what you want from LinkedIn. And that, just like a hammer, helps the carpenter build a house; it's one of the tools that is supercharging your professional life. Read the book. Take action. And I'll see you on LinkedIn.

—David J.P. Fisher, author of *Networking in the 21ˢᵗ Century...* on LinkedIn

https://www.linkedin.com/in/iamdfish/

Introduction

Let's get this out of the way right up front: We believe LinkedIn is the best platform for professionals and businesses. That said, we also acknowledge that LinkedIn is probably one of the most misunderstood and misused platforms.

People find LinkedIn confusing because they view it as a social media platform instead of a social networking platform. LinkedIn is a social **networking** platform.

LinkedIn has grown to over 700 million members in over 200 countries worldwide from its humble beginnings in Reid Hoffman's living room. According to LinkedIn, LinkedIn is one of the most actively used social platforms, with more than 40% of all monthly active users on the platform daily.

An estimated 61 million LinkedIn members are senior-level influencers, and 40 million are in decision-making positions, which means whether you are a job seeker, executive, or business owner, the people you need to find are probably on the platform.

Unlike other social media sites—YouTube and Facebook, for example—the vast majority of companies allow LinkedIn to be used by their employees. For you, this means your potential audience is on LinkedIn and thinking business during business hours.

Are you using LinkedIn to its full potential?

There's an excellent chance nearly everyone you run into has a LinkedIn profile. However, there's a big difference between being on LinkedIn versus using LinkedIn. You can leverage LinkedIn in many different ways:

- Building trust, authority, and credibility
- Finding jobs
- Hiring
- Generating and capturing leads
- Building your business or personal brand
- Gaining industry knowledge
- Consuming content
- Creating content (thought leadership)
- Finding support
- Networking
- Targeting decision-makers
- Curating content
- Getting noticed
- Finding support/collaborating

And the list goes on. However, before you can take full advantage of LinkedIn, you need to know why you want to be on the platform in the first place. Once you have clarity around your purpose on the platform, you'll be able to turn LinkedIn into your personal and business brand-building, lead-generating machine!

What Do You Want to Be Known For?

Do you know what you want to be known for? (Yes, I know you shouldn't end a sentence with a preposition.) More specifically, what do you want your customers/clients to know you for? What do you want potential hiring managers to know you for?

Before you can make the most of LinkedIn **[Strategy #1],** you need to know the answer to this question because your audience will be looking for this when they review your profile. If you don't know the answer to the question, how will your audience figure it out?

Knowing what you want to be known for impacts the effectiveness of your messaging and marketing efforts on LinkedIn. Without an answer to this question, you'll waste time, and will quickly become "that guy or gal" as you try to figure out what to do.

As Jane Anderson, a personal branding expert in Australia, says, "It's one thing to know something; it's quite another to be known for knowing something."

So, are you:

- A branding expert?
- A marketing expert?
- A product manager?
- A resume writer?
- An accountant?

What do you want to be known for? Far too many people fail to ask this question, but the answer is *the* key to your personal and professional success. If you are struggling with this, **[Strategy #2]** here's a quick and easy exercise to help.

1 - List your skills.
2 - Write down your experiences.
3 - List the problem you solve with items 1 and 2.

Once finished, you'll understand what you **could** become known for if you implement the steps in this book.

Know Your Goals

People go astray on LinkedIn (or other social platforms, for that matter) because they are not sure why they are on the platform. You may have created a profile, and that's it, but to be successful, **[Strategy #3]** you need to determine your LinkedIn goals.

Many people see others having success on LinkedIn and think, *Hey, maybe I should get on LinkedIn too.* So, they create a profile and quickly fall victim to random activities, poor messaging, and worse, connecting with every single person who shows an interest. As a result, they get frustrated, curse the system, and abandon it. If this sounds like you, the problem is not you. It's a lack of understanding of the platform and a lack of goals. So, take a minute and jot both down.

Why do you want to be on LinkedIn (your purpose)?

What are your goals for the platform (be specific)?

Answering these questions will give you clarity and create a better overall experience for everyone. Before we dive into the LinkedIn Made Simple process, take a minute, and consider everything we've discussed at this point.

- You know your skills.
- You know your experiences.
- You know the problems you solve.

These three things taken together will help you understand what you want to be known for. Now let's add to that your goals and purpose. Pull it all together, and you've got a blueprint for positioning yourself in the best and most authentic way on LinkedIn.

Andy's Guide to LinkedIn Etiquette

Before diving in, we feel it's necessary to provide some ground rules for your LinkedIn interactions. Here are our guidelines distilled into simple dos and don'ts.

DO THIS

(1) Do build up social capital before you try to spend it.

When you are asked to help someone, and you come through, you've gained an ally. You've earned a favor, which you can potentially call in at a later date. Therefore, it makes sense to look for ways to help people, whether it's making introductions to your network, sharing their posts, giving them advice, or lifting them up in some way. By helping as many different people as possible on your professional journey, you're digging your well before you're thirsty.

(2) Do comment, like, and share.

Suppose you're wondering why no one is visiting your profile, or you're frustrated your posts don't seem to get any traction. In that case, it's partly because you are not participating in the many conversations taking place around you. Dive in and engage! When you do, you'll be making new acquaintances, having fun, and at the same time, seeding engagement and building brand awareness.

(3) Do take good care of your LinkedIn profile.

If you don't have a photo or the photo is low quality, or you don't bother to write a good summary, or you have not added enough detail in your Experience section, or the rich media you've added looks crappy, people will assume that you are not taking your

LinkedIn brand seriously. Why, then, should they take you seriously?

(4) Do engage with your friends and your audience.

Everyone who comments on your content is your friend. When you don't respond to their comments with a comment or a like, you'll lose a friend. Ignoring comments harms your reach; the algorithm is watching to see if you engage, will reward it when you do, ding your reach if you don't. Your audience is always there for you. They're the first to share your content, and they're always commenting. Embrace your audience and ensure they know how much you cherish and appreciate them. They chose to promote you, and they're doing it for free. Please pay them in kindness.

(5) Do keep your network visible to all of your connections.

If you hide your network, expect your connections to hide theirs too. That's a lose-lose for everyone. If you are worried about competitors nosing around your network, simply don't connect with competitors in the first place. Don't penalize the rest of your network because of this easily isolated and distant threat.

(6) Do say "Thank you," and if you wish, reciprocate when a connection endorses you.

This is just good manners. An endorsement is merely a professional thumbs-up, a sign that you have a network that cares about and supports you. If you're given an endorsement you don't feel is appropriate, simply hide it. Don't make a fuss; it is not that big of a deal. If someone endorses you, they tried to do something nice for you—let's not lose sight of that.

(7) Do ensure your profile is up to date and strive to be authentically presented.

Nothing says authenticity more than having a current photo. As a test, would someone recognize you by looking at your picture if you walked into the room right now? I used to have an old photo of a younger, leaner me on LinkedIn, and I had to ditch it because it wasn't who I am now. Keep it real.

(8) Do read all comments before commenting.

I do this instinctively, and I can tell when others don't. They'll make similar or precisely the same points, and they'll be perceived as someone who is not paying attention, ignorant, or worse, self-important. It's the equivalent of barging into a conversation without listening or acknowledging what's already been said. Rude! Recognizing others, their perspective, and building on a conversation topic is the most effective way to dialogue in real life and on LinkedIn. It's hard to read all comments on a popular post, especially if they're in the triple digits. In this scenario, try to read the "top comments" to get a good gist of what's already been said.

(9) Do show situational awareness.

You can now tell if a connection is on the mobile or desktop version of LinkedIn (solid green dot = desktop, green ring = mobile). By acknowledging this, you kick engagement up a notch. "Hey Roneen, I can see that you're mobile right now. Let's continue our discussion when you're back at your desk."

*(10) Do change **Press Enter to Send** to **Click Send** in LinkedIn messaging.*

[Strategy #4] Doing this will prevent embarrassing incomplete/confusing communication. It is natural to click enter when typing paragraphs; it is not natural to click enter to send messages. LinkedIn should remove the first, unnatural option. I see this faux pas happening all the time, and it is an unfortunate but avoidable user error. To set this, click the three dots in the message box to open the window below and select the *Click Send* option.

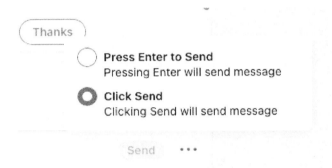

(11) Do connect with followers.

People who follow you are connections waiting to be asked. They made the first move; your job is to take the next step. Look for commonality, elements such as people, places, roles, or interests you share.

(12) Do browse, return browse, and if appropriate, connect.

One of the reasons I'm on LinkedIn is to develop a mutually supportive network. **[Strategy #5]** The best way to build this is by paying close attention to everyone who engages with me or my content. When I browse someone, and they return browse, that's an opportunity to engage and to have a conversation. If someone browses me, I will return browse within two to four hours.

This shows that I am attentive and signals that I am potentially receptive to communication. Rapid, reciprocal, and proactive are the hallmarks of a smart social engagement strategy. If you don't live on LinkedIn like me, get into the habit of checking in at least once a day. At a minimum, return browse those profile visitors that intrigue you, accept relevant connection requests, and respond to your messages.

(13) Do your homework before you approach anyone on LinkedIn.

Review their **All Activity** section before writing that short, ultra-relevant, and well-informed custom connection request. If someone is moderately active on LinkedIn, you'll be able to see what they engage in, what they're interested in, and where their focus lies. I tell my clients All Activity can be a veritable gold mine of useful information, and it should be the first and last thing you review before meeting and trying to engage with anyone in real life. These days, not doing this kind of person-centric research puts you at a distinct disadvantage. It should be pretty obvious that you are wasting your time when you send that no-research connection request.

(14) Do build your network in an intelligent, meaningful, and strategic manner.

[**Strategy #6**] I look for a "tell" and several mutual areas of interest when connecting. If they have 500+ connections, this tells me that they're open to building their virtual network. If they're in my home city (Chicago), there's a strong chance of meeting in real life. If we share a function or work in the same field or have a high number of first-degree connections in common, there are multiple good reasons to connect and build a network with strong foundations.

(15) Do use your time on LinkedIn wisely.

[**Strategy #7**] If you're spending your precious time "pruning" your network to weed out people you think are not going to help you, or you're trying to hide your network, you're wasting your time. Other time-wasting activities include getting into public spats, touching toxic content, clicking *I don't know this person,* debating controversial subjects, sending pitches soon after connecting, and mistaking LinkedIn for Facebook. For these and other don'ts, read on.

DON'T DO THIS

(16) Don't harass or be a pest.

Don't send communications commenting on or complimenting women on their looks, asking about their status, or asking them out for coffee/lunch/dinner. LinkedIn is not Tinder, match.com, or Ashley Madison. If you act like it is, don't be surprised when you are publicly called out by any of your chosen unlucky female targets. You earned the vilification and shame by not keeping it professional. A friend of mine no longer displays her photo because she was sick and tired of the constant odious, knuckle-dragger attention, a sad commentary on what some women have to endure. After all, some men are dumb and lecherous.

(17) Don't comment on bikini, risqué, or NSFW (not safe for work) content.

Even if you think it's harmless, fun, provocative, or edgy, there's a strong chance that someone connected and perhaps pivotal to you will find it offensive. **[Strategy #8]** And above all—don't comment to criticize anyone who shared/commented. Let it slide on by, pretend you didn't see it in your content feed. Treat it like toxic waste and don't touch it in any way. If you do comment, potentially everyone in your network will see the original post juxtaposed with your comments; they won't necessarily read your comments. Still, they may think that you exercised poor judgment by being associated with it in any way. LinkedIn is a business-focused platform, so think boardroom rather than a bar.

(18) Don't get drawn into vociferous, ill-natured public debates (arguments).

If a discussion turns heated, don't get sucked in. Don't respond with that witty put-down. Just go somewhere else, walk away, and cool off. You can do real damage to your professional brand by going toe-to-toe with another professional in a public forum. There's a crowd gathering on the virtual sidewalk. They are there, but you can't see them. They're taking notes, and they're judging.

(19) Don't discuss politics or religion.

LinkedIn is a great place to engage, learn, and build new relationships. **[Strategy #9]** Most people prefer to keep their political views and religious beliefs to themselves. A debate, friendly or otherwise, about either of these divisive subjects, is unlikely to change long-held opinions and beliefs or add value or light, so focus instead on ties that bind rather than things we don't and will likely never have in common.

(20) Don't use auto-visit, marketing campaigns, or social selling software bots.

[Strategy #10] LinkedIn requires a human touch to be done well. If you outsource tasks like profile visits to software programs, you forfeit the right to defend yourself against account suspension or deletion. I won't say this is the inevitable consequence, but I will say that the risk is real and too great. There's cutting corners, and there's cutting your nose off to spite your face.

(21) Don't write clickbait or frothy, no-value content.

Clickbait is two visible lines of text in an update designed to get readers to click. If you fail to deliver or squander your attention opportunity, then expect to be ignored the next time you post—empty calories. Try to give the literary equivalent of a filet or porterhouse. Don't write an airport sub sandwich with all of the contents on display and nothing in the dry, unappetizing middle.

(22) Don't say you're done and then fail to follow through.

I've observed quite a few tantrum posts where the author has decided to throw his toys out of the pram. You may have seen these too: "Why I'm Quitting LinkedIn," "Good-Bye LinkedIn," "LinkedIn, I've Had Enough." I certainly can understand the frustration that erupts from time to time when using LinkedIn. Still, I've never understood the dramatic exit declaration, which always, *always* ends up as a lie or a second act. When people do this kind of grandstanding, they subsequently lose credibility by hanging around or creeping back to the platform they left in a hissy fit.

(23) Don't send boilerplate messages. Don't sell.

Now and again, someone connects with me and immediately sends a message that has clearly been copied and pasted a thousand times. It feels scripted and forced. Don't do that. Create a personalized message that refers to something we have in common, or a topic discussed recently. Start that critical first conversation in a natural, organic way. Don't sound and act like a robot, don't pitch me on your services. I will never agree to a short conversation to "find out more about what you do." This simply confirms you don't know anything about me or my line of work.

(24) Don't stalk by accident.

[Strategy #11] Check and close any open tabs if you happen to be on someone's profile. Check settings to see where you are logged into LinkedIn and log out of those other active sessions. You could appear in their browsing history without realizing it. Logging out of those other sessions is also a simple yet effective security protocol.

(25) Don't tag other users unless you think they'll respond.

Use past experience as a guide. If they previously engaged on the same or a similar topic, then it should be relevant. If someone removes their tag, take note, and don't tag them again. If you're trying to engage Influencers by tagging, understand that the likelihood of getting a response is slim because Influencers with hundreds of thousands of followers are inundated with tag notifications daily. Tag those Influencers who are known to engage and are receptive to tagging.

(26) Don't connect with someone just because they have a pulse.

[Strategy #12] Be strategic and tactical when developing your network. Don't pursue an open network or LION connection methodology. Aim for quality, not quantity, when building virtual relationships. When you connect with anybody and everybody, you're left with a disorganized phonebook instead of a valuable Rolodex.

(27) Don't click IDK or report anyone for spam when they reach out to connect with you.

Just click *Ignore* and refrain from taking the extra, unnecessary punitive step of reporting them. You don't know them; you don't need to hobble them. I've always considered the IDK/spam reporting option as spiteful and mean-spirited. Live and let live. I fully expect LinkedIn to remove this nasty reproach.

(28) Don't troll or feed trolls.

[Strategy #13] Don't be obnoxious. If you can't say something nice, say nothing at all. If you disapprove of language or find certain words offensive, don't criticize or chastise; just move on. Some users will go out of their way to annoy or provoke you. Some will just be content to see their provocation in print. Don't give them any oxygen or time. Either ignore them or delete/report their comments, and if you feel it is warranted, block them.

(29) Don't overshare.

A frequent criticism I hear is that LinkedIn is becoming too personal. You got married. You became a father. You just walked on hot coals. Your dog died yesterday. Most people really don't care. It's not that they're heartless. It's because they're on LinkedIn to make progress, add/grab insights, and build their brand. **[Strategy #14]** If you've got a burning desire to share personal content, then do it. But don't do it because you feel that you have to churn out a post or an update every day just to be present. A good rule of thumb is to write when you have something valuable to share. Are you saying something different, unique, and important? Are you focused on your core skills, talent, and experience? If your engagement stats are in a slow death spiral, it's usually a good indicator that you're oversharing and not delivering value or relevance to your network.

(30) Don't send a connection request without customizing.

I'd rather say "Let's!" than send no message at all. Don't say "I stumbled across your profile" when connecting. It makes you sound like you are literally stumbling through life. Say something like "I was researching X on LinkedIn and found you" or "I was exploring Y, and this led me to you." Be deliberate and strategic instead of haphazard and accidental. You want the recipient to accept your invitation, right? Then spend the time to say why they should.

Links and Profiles Mentioned

PROFILES

- Ryan Rhoten – https://www.linkedin.com/in/ryanrhoten/
- Andy Foote – https://www.linkedin.com/in/andyfoote/

PART 1

Connect

Identify Your Audience

Your Ideal Audience

To get the most from LinkedIn, **[Strategy #15]** you MUST know your ideal audience. Your ideal audience will vary according to your goals. A job seeker's audience may be hiring managers or recruiters, while a business owner may be looking for an audience for their products or services.

Fortunately, identifying your ideal audience is simple. Unfortunately, it's not easy. As you go through this section and consider your audience, some things will come to you naturally, while other things will require you to do some investigation.

So, who is your ideal audience? If you're having trouble visualizing someone, think about the problems you are uniquely qualified to solve. Who has those problems? As a reference, Ryan's ideal audience is Mary. Mary is a business owner who struggles to find clarity in how she positions, packages, and promotes her business.

OK, your turn. Write down your ideal audience's name or job title:

Note to job seekers. As you work through this book, it will help if you consider yourself a business of one, as my friend Mark Anthony Dyson suggested on Ryan's podcast. Generally speaking, your audience is the hiring manager and the HR manager at your target company.

Audience Insights

Understanding your target audience is a bit more straightforward if you're a business. If you are a personal brand completing this exercise, think about yourself as a business of one. Like a business, you are hired to solve problems for the company using your skill set. Whether you are a business or a personal brand you need to understand certain aspects of your ideal audience such as demographics and insights.

Demographics

Demographics are quantifiable pieces of information about your target audience. Demographics include age, race, ethnicity, gender, marital status, children, income, education, locations, and employment. Most of these things you probably already know about your target audience. **[Strategy #16]**. Demographics are essential for two reasons. First, they paint a picture of your audience, and second, demographics are needed for advertising.

As an example of how to use demographics when identifying your audience, Ryan's audience, Mary, is between thirty and forty years old. She is married with at least one child. For the most part, Mary lives in the United States, but she can just as easily be a global citizen. She is college-educated and self-employed. Mary is usually a coach, consultant, or a business owner with no or a small team. Are you starting to picture Mary?

Now it's your turn. For your ideal audience, capture the following information.

Name:

Location:

Age:

Gender:

Education:

Degree:

Field of Study:

School:

Employee: Yes or No

An employee is a person employed by a company and is paid for their skills.

Function (department):

Level (seniority in the organization):

Title:

NOTE: *Titles can be nebulous and vary from company to company. If you're not careful, they can lead you down the wrong path. For example, there are varying levels of the title president, so be as specific as you need to capture the right audience. We'll discuss this in detail in the Search chapter.*

Skills:

Years of Experience:

Income:

Language:

Employer? Yes or No

Annual Revenue:

What type of company is it?

Is it private, public, nonprofit?

What industry are they in?

The number of employees:

Do they follow specific companies (Apple, Target)?

Interests

One area commonly overlooked when determining your ideal audience is their Interests. **[Strategy #17]** To get in front of your audience, you need to understand their interests. So, take a minute and list out the following for your target audience.

General Interests (technology, marketing, sales):

Associations:

Publications they read:

Organizations they belong to:

Brands they follow:

Events they attend:

TV shows do they watch:

Social media platforms are they use:

Groups they belong to:

We'll cover groups in more detail in a later chapter, but they are a great place to find and connect with your ideal audience.

Keywords and Skills

While not exactly a search engine, LinkedIn is like Google for 700 million-plus business professionals, which means you need to understand the keywords or phrases others use when searching for solutions to their problems.

Keywords, as Google defines them are: *"An informative word used in an information retrieval system to indicate the content of a document."* When someone uses a search engine, they type into the search bar a keyword or phrase. The search engine then returns a list of things—in LinkedIn's case, people or companies related to the keyword you entered. If your ideal audience is looking for a solution to a problem, what would they search for?

Capture those keywords, key phrases, or skills:

[Strategy #18] The keywords you list need to align with the skills you possess to help your audience solve their problems. A great place to find keywords is in the headline or titles of personal profiles. How do people in your ideal audience refer to themselves?

Links and Profiles Mentioned

PROFILES

* Mark Anthony Dyson - https://www.linkedin.com/in/markanthonydyson/

Craft Your Story

Positioning

Before moving forward, you need to step back. Don't worry, you're not going far, just to the previous chapter and your answer to the question: What do you want to be known for? The answer to this question helps determine your positioning. How you position yourself on LinkedIn for your business or career is the difference between bringing opportunities to you or having them go to someone else. Positioning consists of three components.

1. **Your goals:** What are you trying to achieve? Why are you on LinkedIn?
2. **Your audience:** Whom do you want to work with?
3. **Your story (message):** What do you want people to know about you?

As Andy mentioned, whether you like it or not, you are judged every day. People judge you based on your clothes, actions, behaviors, online profiles, and yes, even your LinkedIn profile. If your positioning is not clear, people will be confused about what you do and how you help. You can avoid this by crafting a unique story for your brand.

Tell Your Story

[Strategy #19] When telling your story, it helps to break it down into smaller parts, then put it back together in a logical manner to define your positioning. When written correctly, as your audience reads your profile, they should be able to picture themselves in your story. A common mistake is focusing on yourself and not on your ideal audience. To help with this, break down your story into individual parts, starting with a situation.

Situation

To pull your audience into your story, you need to start with a situation they will understand. For example, you know your audience wants to achieve something, but they need help, so your story needs to let them know you understand their situation and how you can help them achieve their goals. As an example, assume you're a digital marketer and your target audience wants to generate more leads with their website. Imagine the situation the person responsible for generating leads at the company is in. By thinking about their situation, you put yourself in their shoes, which makes it much easier to think through the relevant details.

Questions to answer:

What goal(s) are they trying to achieve?

What do they want to accomplish?

Obstacles

If your audience could achieve their goals on their own, they wouldn't need help. Fortunately for you, they can't, so they need **your** help. After identifying the situation your audience is facing, now you need to consider the obstacles preventing them from achieving their goals. Obstacles can range from technical ones to a lack of knowledge. Businesses hire people (job seekers) or contract businesses to help them overcome their obstacles.

Question: What obstacles is your audience facing?

Feelings

Once you know the obstacles, next you need to understand how those obstacles make your audience feel. Are they frustrated, upset, angry, mad, embarrassed? According to an article written by Logan Chierotti, published on INC.com (1), "humans are driven by feelings." Specifically, emotions, and "emotion is what drives purchasing behaviors and decision making in general." With this in mind, how do the obstacles your audience is facing make them feel? **[Strategy #20]** Understanding this helps you relate to your audience's situation by demonstrating empathy in your story.

Question: How do the obstacles my audience is facing make them feel?

Experiences

To build trust with your audience, you need to relate your experiences to their situation. Saying something as simple as, "I understand what it's like," or "Hey, I get what you're going through because I've been there and done that" is often enough to help people recognize you've experienced what they are going through.

Question: How do you let your audience know you understand their situation?

Credibility

Tying your experiences to your audience's situation helps you build a connection with them. Now you need to demonstrate your credibility. A great way to do this is through certifications. Certifications prove you understand a specific topic or discipline. Some credentials even allow you to borrow others' authority.

Questions:

What are your relevant certifications?

Action

We can't resolve anything without taking action. As your audience looks for a solution, they will be more apt to look in your direction if you guide them. The best way to guide anyone is to provide them with the steps or actions needed to achieve their goals.

Question: What steps did you take in a similar situation to help your audience achieve their goals?

Consequences

Your audience will typically not take action if there are no consequences. In other words, if they do nothing about their situation, it may continue to get worse. Your experience helps them avoid the consequences of inaction.

Question: What do you help your audience avoid?

Accomplishments

As stated in the Situation paragraph above, your audience is trying to achieve, or accomplish a goal. Your story should paint the picture of how you've helped others get past their obstacles, avoid the consequences of inaction, and achieve their goals. Be clear on the accomplishments you help your audience obtain. State them clearly and use percentages, numbers, or dollars whenever possible. Testimonials help as well. It's one thing to say you helped a company increase its leads. It's another thing entirely when you can say you helped a company increase their leads by 200%.

Question: What do you help your audience achieve?

Assemble Your Story

[Strategy #21] Write down your answers to the previous questions in the order they were presented. Sticking with the digital marketer scenario, your story might look like this:

Situation – Your audience wants to get more leads from their website.

Obstacle – They don't know the right tactics or strategy to capture more leads.

Feelings – This frustrates them because they feel like they should know how to do this, and their boss is applying pressure to get this done quickly.

Experience – You understand this situation because you've seen others struggle with this as well.

Credibility – As a certified digital marketer, you've experienced similar situations and helped clients capture more leads from their websites.

Actions – First, analyzing their website. Second, identifying key opportunities to improve. Third, you implemented the required strategies.

Consequences – You helped them avoid losing out on additional leads.

Achievements – You helped them capture 200% more leads in the first thirty days.

All Together

My audience wants to capture more leads from their website. Unfortunately, they don't know how, which is frustrating because they are under pressure to perform. As a certified digital marketer, I've helped resolve similar situations by analyzing the website and identifying areas for improvement. Implementing the required actions has helped my audience avoid losing new leads, and instead, they've been able to capture 200% more leads in the first thirty days after working with me.

Now you have a baseline story you can use throughout your profile. You can use this same methodology to structure your About section and each of your experience sections.

Links and Profiles Mentioned

LINKS

- (1) https://www.inc.com/logan-chierotti/harvard-professor-says-95-of-purchasing-decisions-are-subconscious.html

PROFILES

- Jane Anderson - https://www.linkedin.com/in/janeandersonpersonalbranding/

Your Pitch

There is one question both business owners and job seekers hate. This question raises blood pressure and anxiety levels simultaneously. The question is phrased differently depending on whether you are a business owner or a job seeker, but the effect is the same. The question is:

What do you do?

Or...

Tell me about yourself.

Did reading those questions send shivers down your spine? If so, you're not alone. This question is difficult to answer for two reasons. First, you're being asked to consolidate your entire career/business into a semi-short answer. Second, it's very easy to answer this question with a nonstop parade of sentences. Fortunately, it doesn't have to be this way if you follow the pitch framework.

The Framework

This framework will help you nail this question every time. You will need to refer to your answers from the previous chapter to complete this exercise. *Note to job seekers: In the following example, substitute the word client(s) with an appropriate response.*

[Strategy #22] The framework looks like this: Obstacles + Solution + Success.

Obstacles

Start your answer with an obstacle your audience is facing. For example, many people struggle with or to [insert obstacle].

"Many people struggle to understand how to use LinkedIn effectively."

Alternatively, you can start with something you know your audience wants to achieve, then mention an obstacle in their way.

"Many people want to use LinkedIn more effectively but struggle to make sense of the platform."

The next part of the framework is to add how the obstacle makes your audience feel, plus any consequences.

"Many people struggle to understand how to use LinkedIn effectively, which is frustrating because they know they are losing clients."

If you've done your research correctly, a statement like the one above will resonate and capture attention. People will want to know what comes next.

Solution

Now, it's time to paint yourself (or business) as the solution. To do that, you need to connect with your prospect using reputation, credibility, and your solution from the previous exercise. The key here is to acknowledge your audience's obstacles. Saying something as simple as "I understand" builds empathy and helps your audience know you understand them. It also positions you to talk about yourself without sounding like you're bragging.

"After working in [insert industry, job title, or role], I understand how frustrating LinkedIn can be, which is why I decided to do something about it [insert what you did or the solution you used]."

This part of the formula will vary based on your solution. Your aim is to position yourself as *the* person (company) who can solve the stated obstacle.

"Many people struggle to understand how to use LinkedIn effectively, which is frustrating because they know they are losing clients.

Having worked with many clients on LinkedIn over the last five years, I understand how confusing LinkedIn can be, which is why I developed LinkedIn Made Simple."

Success

Now you are ready to tell your audience the results of your efforts. At this point, you will state your solution and the accomplishments you achieved. To do this, first, state your solution, then use the phrase, "so that."

"So that" provides a segue to the accomplishments.

"LinkedIn Made Simple is a step-by-step online course designed to take the confusion out of LinkedIn so that you can use it to gain clients."

Put it All Together

When you assemble all of the pieces in the framework, your pitch might sound something like this:

"Many people struggle to understand how to use LinkedIn effectively, which is frustrating because they know they are losing clients.

Having worked with many people on LinkedIn over the last five years, I understand how confusing it can be, which is why I developed LinkedIn Made Simple, a step-by-step online course designed to take the confusion out of LinkedIn so that you can use it effectively to gain clients."

Simple yet effective. The next time you're asked to tell someone what you do, use the pitch formula to compose your answer. You'll be brief to the point and provide a segue into a more directed discussion.

PART 2

Converse

Build Your Profile

If you have skipped to this step without reading the previous chapters or completing the exercises, you've missed 22 strategies, and your profile will **not** be as effective as it could be. That said, let's get started.

Your profile is where you pull together all of your previous work. When done correctly, it's how people viewing your profile can begin to visualize themselves working with you. Everything you've done so far has led you to this point. You've defined your ideal audience, and you've made your story relevant to attract their attention. Before diving into updating your profile, it's essential to understand why you need a customer-facing profile.

Components of a Customer-Facing Profile

At a high-level, your LinkedIn profile is all about positioning and at the heart of positioning is your message. When you update your profile, you are optimizing your message for your target audience to capture their attention. **[Strategy #23]** A focused message consists of three different components: brand, business, benefit.

Brand

The American Marketing Association defines brand as "a name, term, design, symbol, or any other feature that identifies one seller's good or service as distinct from those of other sellers." As Ryan discussed in his book, *CareerKred*, it does not matter if you are an individual or a business entity; you have a brand. You offer "features" (read that as skills) that separate you from others. These skills enable you to add value to your target audience. Your profile allows you to bring awareness to your brand and help people understand who you are and how you help.

Business

From a business standpoint, you need to let people know what you do. Even if you are a personal brand, you are still a business of one, so your profile needs to help viewers understand what you do. Like Google, you get found in LinkedIn via your keywords. Keywords are what people will use when searching for someone on LinkedIn, such as:

- Digital marketing
- Product management
- Brand messaging
- Certified Public Accountant

Benefit

If you don't tell people how you help, they will interpret this on their own. Adding the benefits your target audience experiences when working with you is how you create a customer-facing profile. When you add benefits to your profile, it rounds out your story for your audience. You need all three components—brand, business, and benefit—working together to create a customer-facing profile to capture views from the right people.

The Customer-Facing Profile

Before you start updating your profile, it helps to have available the work you did in the previous chapters. Additionally, you'll want to turn off notifications, so you'll want to double-check this feature is turned off. Otherwise, every time you save an update, your network will get notified.

To turn off notifications, go to **Settings & Privacy.** Under **Visibility,** open **Share job changes, education changes, and work anniversaries from your profile.** Ensure the toggle is set to *No*; this will prevent your network from being notified of your changes. Here are some additional tips to keep in mind when updating your profile.

Tips

[Strategy #24] Your profile may be about you, but it's not for you.

It should be clear by now but, just in case, remember your profile is about you but it's not your resume or a place to put random tasks you do for your job.

Write in first person, not third person.

LinkedIn is a social network, so be social and write in the first person.

Save your work

Save changes to your profile as you go. Make a few changes, save your work, then refresh the page, and you should be good to go.

Use notifications strategically

If you want people to know about your updates after you've completed your profile or before you make your last change, go back to your privacy settings and toggle the **Share job changes** switch to *On*. As soon as you save your profile, a notification will go out to your network. Remember to change the toggle back to *Off* afterward.

There are many reasons to notify your network. You may have taken a new role, moved to a new company, started a business, or a side gig. The point is to use notifications strategically rather than notifying your network anytime you make a small insignificant change to your profile.

Update Your Profile

The following is our recommended sequence to update your profile. **[Strategy #25]** The sequence gives you a structure to follow and makes it easier to keep track of where you are and what you have left to complete.

Your URL

If needed, review and update your URL. By default, LinkedIn adds a string of numbers at the end of your name in the URL. Generally speaking, you can tell by reviewing the URL how active and knowledgeable someone is with the platform.

www.linkedin.com/in/afua-abrafi-2a269743/

www.linkedin.com/in/ryanrhoten/

www.linkedin.com/in/andyfoote/

Fortunately, LinkedIn allows you to change your URL into what is commonly referred to as a vanity URL. We recommend keeping it simple by deleting the string of numbers and making your URL only your name. However, you may not be able to use your name because someone else who shares your name has already claimed the URL. If this happens, here are a few suggestions on what you can do.

- Add a middle initial.
- Add the word "the" in front of your name.
- Add a keyword behind your name (digital marketer, personal branding)

After you've crafted your custom LinkedIn URL, use it liberally. Add it to your email signature and other social channels so people can find you; doing so will boost your profile page visits.

Your Background Image

The next thing to update on your profile is your background image. By default, LinkedIn gives you a generic background. This background does nothing to help brand yourself and sends a message about your knowledge of LinkedIn. Your background image is like a billboard on the highway. Use it to convey information about yourself or your business. Programs like Canva.com or Adobe Spark help you quickly create a background image that will stand out. Here are some great examples:

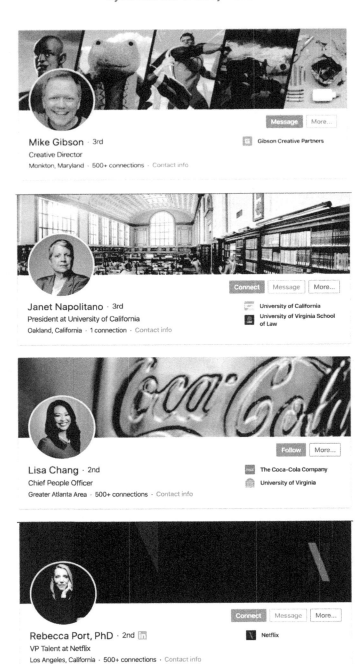

Your Profile Picture (Headshot)

Despite the thousands of written articles and videos on this topic, for whatever reason, people still do not seem to have a grasp on the profile picture, so here are some quick rules for your profile picture.

- No selfies.
- No pictures of you standing 26 feet away from the camera.
- No pictures of you with your family.
- No action-adventure shots.
- No pictures with your significant other.
- No pictures of you with guns (I've seen this too many times to count).
- No pictures of you smoking (anything).

Your LinkedIn profile picture should be current and professional, so have a professional headshot taken and add it to your profile.

Your Name

Your name is, well, your name. If you have a professional designation, like a Ph.D., feel free to include it after your name. You can put nicknames and your maiden name (there's actually a button for this). Keep it simple; make it your name.

Your Headline

The headline may be the most crucial component of your profile. By default, the headline is your current title, which is boring and unfortunate because your headline shows up everywhere. If you publish a post, like, share, or comment on a post, your profile picture and headline are visible. We recommend using keywords in your headline. When somebody searches for something or someone in LinkedIn, they use keywords, so make sure you add keywords into your headline. Feel free to add some personality but remember you only get 220 characters, so use them wisely. Here are a few examples of how you can structure your headline.

OK:
Authority | Title | Skills (keywords)

Title, Company | I help [Industry] [Success]

Title, Company | [Keyword] | [Keyword] | [Keyword]

BETTER:
Title | I help [audience/customer] achieve [success]

Title | I help [audience/customer] to [solve problem] by [your solution/expertise]

I help [audience/customer] do or accomplish [success] through or by [your solution/expertise]

BEST: Add your pitch here
Many [audience/customer] struggle with [obstacle] which is [emotion] which is why [your solution/expertise] so that [success they achieve]

It is okay to use humor if it aligns with your personality. Just be clear on who and how you help. Think about what will capture your audience's attention.

- "I help save you money with solar."
- "I'm the solar energy guy."
- "I'll cut your energy bill by 80%."

Here are examples of people who are fully leveraging the headline space.

Sarah Jones – Helping smart, introverted men attract women naturally.

Bruce Johnston – My clients integrate LinkedIn into their existing sales and marketing processes. The result is more sales.

John Marrett – Helping mid-sized organizations increase sales and improve customer service since 1993 | #linkedinlocal

Kristin A. Sherry – It's hard to read the label when you're inside the jar. YouMap(R) Profile & TalentStory(™) creator. Bestselling author.

Josh Steimle – I turn entrepreneurs into thought leaders. Author, speaker, entrepreneur, husband, dad, skater.

Vatsala Shukla – Empowering, connecting, and supporting Professionals demonstrate Executive Presence, Emotional Intelligence, and Confidence to turn their boring jobs into fulfilling Careers | Executive Coach | Bestselling Author

---

[Strategy #26] Your Name + Headshot + Headline = Your calling card.

These are the three things others will see anytime you view a profile, leave a comment, like something, or are searched for. All three of these things must be helping (and not hurting you). The objective is to get everyone who sees your "calling card" to click on it and visit your profile page.

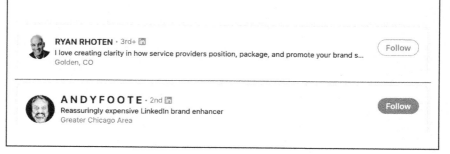

Contact and Personal Information

[Strategy #27] If you want people to contact you, you need to add your personal information. You'd be surprised how many people do not add contact information to their profile. Things you can add here:

- Website links
- Phone number
- Email address
- Your address
- Social accounts
- Your birthday

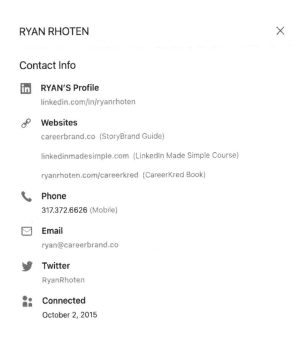

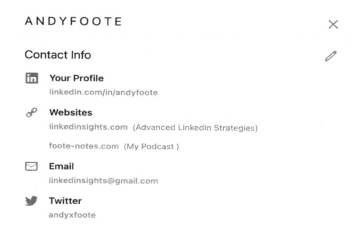

If you are concerned about adding your phone number, we suggest getting a Google Voice number.

Business and Job Seeker Info

LinkedIn has added a section specifically for businesses and job seekers to highlight their areas of expertise. If you're a business, you can add your business focus, and if you're a job seeker, you add work interests here. For job seekers, this feature allows you to let recruiters know you are open to being contacted by them. To enable this feature, go to **Settings & Privacy**. Find **Data Privacy** and **Job-seeking preferences**. Move the toggle to *Yes* to turn this feature on.

The About Section

We wish LinkedIn would call the **About** section "Your Story," because maybe it would help people understand what to put here. Unfortunately, the vast majority of people on LinkedIn leave this section blank or fill it with generic information that could apply to anyone. Either way, it's a huge, missed opportunity. Not only can you tell an engaging story, but the About section is a great place to incorporate your keywords. You get 2,000 characters, not words, to tell your career story. To ensure your success, here are a few recommended guidelines to follow.

[Strategy #28] About Section Guidelines

Write in the first person.

Unless you are a super-famous person, writing in the third person sounds weird.

Tell a story.

Tell your story. Refer back to the situations in the messaging worksheet.

Do not recite your resume.

Even though you put your skills and experiences in your profile, LinkedIn is not your resume.

Additional tips.

If you don't know what to put in your About section, borrow text from your company website. Add your contact details, work email, or work mobile number at the bottom of the About section.

Have fun with it.

LinkedIn allows you to discuss your career in a way a resume or portfolio never could. Your resume is very utilitarian; it doesn't tell anybody how you accomplished what you did. Use your LinkedIn profile to let people know more about who you are, how you add value, and how you go about getting things done. Oh, and please, don't use distracting, unnecessary (and fugly) emojis/weird symbols.

About Section "Methodology"

To help you get started, we've provided a "methodology" for you to write your About section. This is not a copy and paste thing; it's here to help you structure your profile. There are many different ways to approach this section, but the best practice is always telling a story and incorporating your keywords. What follows is a suggested methodology to use when writing your About section.

Example

Start with a situation.

Only the first 200 characters of your About section are visible before your story gets truncated, so you need to capture your audience's attention in those first 200 characters. We suggest using a story (situation) to get started. Highlight an obstacle your audience is struggling with or a question/statement you often hear from people in your target audience.

"I feel like my marketing message is all over the place, and it costs me, clients," she said with a hint of exasperation. After our call, I reflected on how overwhelming marketing is for business owners.

Position yourself as someone who can help.

Build on the situation, share relevant experiences, and expand on your expertise while demonstrating your authority and credibility.

"I realized that [acknowledgment], which is why I [your story on how you got to where you are now]."

OR

"With [X years' experience] solving [problem/obstacle] for [audience], I developed [solution/program], so they can experience [success or accomplishments]."

List out whom you work with or help – OPTIONAL

Continue the story by naming your audience and providing a little detail on how you help. Think about your pitch for reference. You can use all caps to call out this area, but it is not necessary. Example:

CLIENTS I TYPICALLY WORK WITH:

[Audience] - [insert specifics (who you help)] by [insert how you help] so they can [insert success or accomplishment] in [insert time frame if known].

You can also list out successes, your customer's experience, or your value proposition.

- *[success] Save time*
- *[success] Save money*
- *[success] Generate leads*
- *[success] Become a LinkedIn ninja!*

(BTW, never use the word ninja on your profile, unless you legitimately are one, in which case you probably don't need a profile)

How do you help them – Highlight your offering/services

Highlight your products, services, or skills by calling them out. Example:

SERVICES TO DEVELOP YOUR MARKETING MESSAGE

- [service] Digital marketing
- [service] SEO
- [service] StoryBrand guide
- [service] Etc.

End with a Call to Action – Provide a way for people to contact you

State the specific step you want your ideal audience to take next.

- If *you are [audience] and you want to [overcome obstacle], email me at [email address]*.
- *Are you struggling to or with [obstacle]? Then let's talk [insert communication method]*.

You can include other things in your About section, such as testimonials, and quotes from customers/target audience. [**Strategy #29**] Don't write blocks of text. Use short sentences and paragraphs, and remember spaces count as a character. Here are a few good examples of About sections. Notice how they do more than summarize. They don't just talk "about" themselves; they highlight specific key elements of their professional persona.

Ian Sohn

About

As the CEO of Wunderman Thompson Central, I'm responsible for overseeing all agency operations in the Central Region, with a special emphasis on growing new and existing business and expanding the agency's capabilities. The Central Region encompasses nearly 300 people across four offices: Chicago, Minneapolis, Austin and Memphis.

Prior to joining Wunderman Thompson, I was the Managing Director of SapientRazorfish in Chicago where I looked after the business, human and cultural health of the office. I also served as the architect and business lead for a portfolio of brands in categories including CPG, insurance, retail, fashion, pharma and healthcare. Before that, I was the Executive Vice President of Digital and Social at Ogilvy & Mather Worldwide, Inc. in Chicago, where I built and led a team of award-winning digital strategists and founded the agency's award-winning social media practice in 2008. Prior to Ogilvy, I was the global partnership lead for a division of Nokia.

I'm particularly proud of my passion for selling innovative ideas and solutions; the trust my clients put in me; and the joy I take in finding and developing talent. I'm a strong advocate for balance and compassionate leadership in the workplace; writing and speaking about it often.

When I'm not working, I can likely be found chasing my two little boys and puppy, yelling at athletes on TV who can't hear me, watching Keith Moon clips on YouTube, devouring something with ketchup, reading anything I can find on Muhammad Ali, chasing fresh powder on a mountain out west, or running a few miles on the Chicago lakefront.

http://www.iansohn.com

Nanci Smith

About

Growing up on the playgrounds of Detroit, I advocated against child abuse in 4th grade when I discovered my friend's mother would extinguish her cigarettes on her daughter's fingers. By 6th grade, I made an amazing Minestrone for a soup kitchen, only to learn my mom didn't actually know how to get it there.

I developed a thick skin, a quick wit, and a disciplined approach to problem solving by discerning people's interests and motives. I studied Philosophy because the Big Questions matter, and attended law school to fight bullies and injustice.

As a law student, I represented a domestic violence victim through the intimidating world of family court to divorce her batterer. Divorce was foreign to me, as my parents had always been together.

I then became a trial attorney under the apprenticeship of a former attorney general, who taught me the art, skill, and ethics of effective lawyering. A dream called me back to represent the underserved, and I worked at Legal Aid until opening my firm in 2005.

After litigating many custody cases, it gnawed at me that I was contributing to a lifetime of bitterness and resentment for my clients. They were losing so much (time with their children, money, lifestyle, identity) through an aggressive, public and adversarial forum full of shame and blame. I then discovered Collaborative Law (CL).

Clients explore their options, including CL, which is an interdisciplinary and non-adversarial process that empowers clients to make healthy decisions about their post-divorce life.

They put their children's needs ahead of their negative feelings toward their spouse, and choose to act with integrity and decency, despite their pain. Lawyers choose to use collaborative negotiation skills to create a supportive environment to resolve their dispute. It's private, educational, inspirational, and it works.

This is the conflict resolution model that I most value. It recognizes our common humanity.

Let's connect!

Eleni Psaltis

About

"The trouble with law is lawyers."
Clarence Darrow, lawyer and civil libertarian.

Ever the unpopular child, I decided to continue the theme well into adulthood by becoming a lawyer.

Learning the dark arts from the craftiest in the business, first in New Zealand and then abroad, I have now returned home to continue wreaking havoc as an in-house lawyer with post-it notes, red pen and long winded legal documents that no-one really understands (not even myself). My specialties include general commercial law and ICT and looking interested in meetings whilst secretly thinking about lunch.

I may have been known to expedite legal matters in exchange for chocolate and mint condition stationery.

In the words of Jack Nicholson "You can't handle the truth!" And, of course, none of the above is actually true. Or is it...?

< Posts + Articles > I enjoy thinking, writing and sharing information and articles - on being a lawyer, about work, technology, science and whatever else takes my fancy. Sometimes funny, sometimes serious, sometimes cranky. Please do feel free to join in on the conversation, it would be great to hear from you.

Featured Section

The **Featured** section allows you to highlight your expertise, projects, or portfolio your audience may be interested in seeing. You order the items in this section, so they appear how you want them to be displayed. When adding content to the Featured section, consider what is appropriate for your brand.

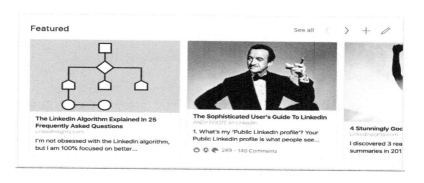

Experiences

The **Experience** section is why most people consider LinkedIn to be a place to post your resume, and it's the most significant missed opportunity for many people. Most profiles on LinkedIn are barebones. Meaning, they probably list their company, a generic job title, and not much else. No descriptions of what they did, achieved, or how they add value. More importantly, no keywords to help them get found in search results.

Like the About section, you can use up to 2,000 characters in each experience section to talk about your role, add some personality, and help people see you as the person who can help them get past their obstacles.

Key Point: The Experience section is where you let your personality show. It is the section where you can expand on your resume bullet points by telling stories about the obstacles you encountered, how you solved problems, and added value to situations.

It's also where you incorporate your keywords, skills, and other relevant terms to help you get found.

[Strategy # 30] Experiences Section Guidelines

Write in First Person

For all the same reasons noted in the About section, tell a story and don't recite your resume. Your goal is to speak to your target audience.

Don't Use a Generic Title

You only get 100 characters for your title. How you structure your title is ultimately up to you, but make sure you incorporate your keywords. If you are struggling with what to write, here are some suggestions to help you start.

I help [audience/customer] achieve [success]

I help [audience/customer] to [solve problem] by [your solution/expertise]

I help [audience/customer] do or accomplish [success] through or by [your solution/expertise]

Authority | Title | Skills (keywords)

Title of company name mission or vision statement

Title, Company | I help [Industry] [Success]

Title, Company | [Keyword] | [Keyword] | [Keyword]

Add Your Location

Include your location. People, potential clients, and hiring managers will search by location.

Break Up Your Text

You want to make your experiences scannable. Write two to three sentences and hit Enter. Your profile will be cleaner in appearance and help people scan it.

Use the About Section Methodology to Structure Your Experiences

Following the same or similar methodology will help you stay consistent with your stories. The Experience section is about individual roles you've held, so start with a situation and tell a story to position yourself as the guide who can help clients or companies overcome their obstacles.

[Strategy # 31] Add Media

At the bottom of each Experience section, you can add media to your profile. Take advantage of this feature. The media you add should support the story you are telling in your text. Think about videos, website links, customer testimonials, and your project portfolio.

Education

Add your education. We recommend leaving your graduation dates blank, and if something is interesting about your education, add it to the description section. For example, Ryan notes in his education section that he's a commercial and instrument-rated pilot.

Licenses and Certifications

Add any relevant licenses or certifications to highlight your authority.

Volunteer

If you have relevant volunteer experience or are just proud of your volunteer experience, add this section to your profile. Volunteerism is an excellent way for you to help your community and be a perfect way for you to round out skill sets you may not be able to get in your current role.

Skills and Endorsements

Speaking of skills, make sure you complete the **Skills and Endorsements** section on your profile. All of the skills you list can help you get found in search. You can add up to fifty skills. Make sure they are relevant to your target audience. You can pin three skills to the top of the list, making it easier for you to get endorsed for them. Most people will not open up the skills section to see what other skills you have listed.

Recommendations

Recommendations are testimonials from others validating what you do and provide proof you can do what you say you can do. If you don't have any recommendations, ask for them. When you write a recommendation for someone, remember you don't just bear the responsibility to do right by your former colleague or client, but you also have an opportunity to express yourself. It doesn't matter if you write 85 or 285 words; just make every single word matter. A great recommendation reflects well on both parties. Take a look at how well Dan Hill (on behalf of

Chiara) and Daniel Lilly (on behalf of Ronald Gerlach) utilize the **Recommendation** feature:

Chiara Sambonet
Planning Director at AKQA
October 29, 2018, Dan
managed Chiara directly

When Chiara gets her hands on a problem you end up feeling sorry for the problem; she's tenacious, intelligent and hugely passionate. She always stood out as one of the most creatively minded and able planners at AKQA. She leans into solving the problem not just defining it well. I loved working with her from day one. Well actually from day two. On day one she also mistook me for a new intern, which I hope, says more about my radiant skin than my gravitas. See less

Ronald Gerlach, PCM
Marketing Director ◆ Digital
Marketing Strategist ◆
Creative Strategy & Brand
Positioning ◆ SEO Ads &
Analytics
September 5, 2010, Ronald
worked with Daniel in the same
group

You can look at Ron Gerlach's book to know that he's a gifted writer who sees opportunities others miss. What you can't get from a portfolio is what it's like to work with Ron every day.

It's insufferable.

For starters, the guy has this knack for asking the question you didn't think of. In itself, that's not a big deal, until it invariably leads to an approach that would have been inconceivable without that perspective or that data point.

Especially if you're the one who has to re-do the PowerPoint.

Then there's the way he talks to clients. It's like he cares about their business results instead of just selling his favorite idea or creating ads that make other agencies jealous. At first you'll think it's just another ad guy defending the work. But then he actually starts collaborating and making the work better.

It's embarrassing.

His office was another sore spot. A lot of creative-types populate their desks and walls with their greatest award-winning or buzz-worthy work. It goes over great on the new-client office tour. Ron, however, insisted on surrounding himself with work in-progress. It was like he'd rather think about the current challenge than dwell on his past successes.

Not even trying, really.

Finally, I need to address Ron's work habits. As if it's not enough that he comes up with the strategy point or the angle or creates the ad that allows you to make your number – everybody's happy when you make the number, right? Not Ron. When you get to the office in the morning – every morning – he's there. First one in and already at work on the next project, objective, campaign, opportunity.

That's just showing off. See less

41

Accomplishments

Accomplishments boost your authority and credibility. They show you are active in your career or Industry. Unlike the accomplishments listed in your Experience section and on your resume, accomplishments listed here fall into one of eight categories. If any of these categories are relevant for you, add them to your profile.

- Publications
- Patents
- Courses
- Projects
- Honors and Awards
- Test scores
- Languages
- Organizations

Interests

The **Interests** section is perhaps the most underutilized section of your LinkedIn profile. Here's why we like the Interests section: it helps people understand you. **[Strategy #32]** The Interests section is a great place to review when completing the ideal audience exercise. Visit someone's profile in your ideal audience and check their interests.

The Interest section becomes even more valuable when we get to the part of this book on messaging. You'll be able to use some of the information here as a way to connect with somebody you don't think you can connect with today.

[Strategy #33] A quick note on the "formulas" noted in this section. Don't take them verbatim. Instead, use them as guidelines.

Links and Profiles Mentioned

PROFILES

- Mike Gibson - https://www.linkedin.com/in/gcpmike/
- Janet Napolitano - https://www.linkedin.com/in/janetnapolitano/
- Lisa Chang - https://www.linkedin.com/in/lisavchang/
- Rebecca Port - https://www.linkedin.com/in/rebeccaport/
- Ian Sohn - https://www.linkedin.com/in/iansohn/
- Nanci Smith - https://www.linkedin.com/in/nanciasmith/
- Eleni Psaltis - https://www.linkedin.com/in/elenipsaltis/
- Sarah Jones - https://www.linkedin.com/in/sarahjones0/
- Bruce Johnston - https://www.linkedin.com/in/brucejohnston115/
- John Barrett - https://www.linkedin.com/in/jmarrett/
- Kristin Sherry - https://www.linkedin.com/in/kristinsherry/
- Josh Steimle - https://www.linkedin.com/in/joshuasteimle/
- Vatsala Shukla - https://www.linkedin.com/in/vatsalashukla/
- Chiara Sambonet - https://www.linkedin.com/in/chiara-sambonet
- Ronald Gerlach - https://www.linkedin.com/in/ronald-gerlach/

Create a Company Page

If you are a personal brand, you should know that company pages are not just for companies. Even if you are an employee with no aspirations of starting a business, there is still some valuable information in this section you can use to enhance your LinkedIn experience. Company pages are great for freelancers, solopreneurs, personal brands with a side gig, authors, and of course, businesses.

Company pages help you in all three areas discussed previously: brand, business, and benefit. As you may recall, Brand is focused on bringing awareness to your brand, so people understand who you are and what you want to be known for. From a business standpoint, your company page will help people understand what you do. And of course, you need to tell people the benefits they will experience from working with you. Your company page helps boost your business in all three areas. There are also some additional benefits to having a company page.

Benefits of Company Pages

1 – They allow you to run ads on LinkedIn.

2 – They provide an additional place for relevant keywords.

If your company page is tied to your personal page, you get to continue to tell your story on your company page.

3 – You can cross-promote content.

For example, you could post something on your profile then repost it to your company page and vice versa. **[Strategy #34]** Cross-promotion is a way to raise brand awareness. More on this strategy later.

4 – You can post open positions to your company page.

5 – You can create showcase pages for your products and services.

Also known as affiliated pages, **[Strategy #35]** showcase pages allow you to talk about the benefits of specific products or services you offer. We'll cover showcases pages a little later.

6 - You can add a logo to your page.

Without a company page, your business's logo will be the generic grey image of a building. **[Strategy #36]** Once you have a company page, you can select your company from your page, and your logo will appear on your personal profile.

Creating Your Page

To create your company page, go to your profile, and find the menu item on the top right side with nine little dots and the word *work* below. Click on the dropdown arrow to open a menu on the right-hand side. You will see **Create a Company Page** with a plus sign at the menu's bottom. Select this item, and you will be redirected to another window to create your company page.

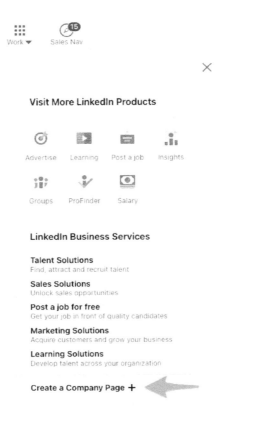

Getting Started

The first thing you need to do when creating a company page is to select the type of page you're making. You'll be presented with the following four options.

- Small business – Fewer than 200 employees
- Med-large business – More than 200 employees
- Showcase page – Sub-page associated with an existing page
- Educational Institution – Colleges and universities

After selecting your page type, you will be able to enter your company's basic information.

The following are things you will enter before proceeding. Having this information available will expedite this part but remember you can change all of this later.

- Page identity: Enter your company name
- Page URL: If you want it to be something different than your company name
- Company website: The URL of your website
- Company industry
- Company size
- Company type
- Your logo

After you verify you are authorized to create your company page, click *Create Page* at the bottom, and you now have a company page.

Updating Your Page

When updating your page, you'll notice many similarities to updating your profile. The main difference is you only need one dialog box to update most things on the page. *Hint:* It helps to have these items prewritten or readily available, so this exercise becomes a simple copy and paste operation. There are three areas for you to update: the cover image, header information, and the About section.

Cover Image

Add a cover image to represent your brand. At the time of publishing this book, the correct cover image size is 1,128px by 191px. You can use a program like Canva to create your image.

Header Section

The header section contains two critical updates: your company details and the button at the top of your page. You'll be able to add or change the following items here.

Company Details

- Your logo
- Company name
- Tagline – Use keywords if possible

Button Details

Select what you want your button to display. Your options for the button include the following:

- Visit Website
- Contact Us
- Learn More
- Register
- Sign Up

About Section

The company page About section is like the About section on your profile. You get 2,600 characters to tell your company story. Use the same framework from your personal page, and be sure to include keywords. If you are a smaller company, say up to twenty-five employees, speak in the first person. For over twenty-five employees, writing in the third person is acceptable. The company page About section consists of an overview, locations, hashtags, and featured groups.

Overview

The **Overview** section is similar to your profile About section. You get 200 characters to talk about how your company benefits its audience. We recommend writing your description in advance, so you can copy and paste it into the box provided. The Overview allows you to add the following information as well:

- Website
- Company Phone
- Company Industry
- Company Size

Locations

Since many people search for services in their local area, LinkedIn allows you to add your local address and the addresses of all your company locations. If you operate your business from home, we suggest getting an address from a local FedEx or UPS store. With either company, you get a real address instead of a P.O. box.

Hashtags

Like hashtags on other social media platforms, LinkedIn uses them to help users find and categorize relevant content quickly. The latest algorithm research points to between three and nine hashtags as the ideal number if you want to maximize reach. We suggest using two "regular" hashtags and one branded (or custom) hashtag for your company page. Hashtags allow your content to be found by others, which will boost your views and lead to higher engagements. Once you've selected which hashtags to follow (you can change these at any time), you will get notified about trending posts using the same hashtags.

#andydoeslinkedin
726 followers

Following

Your notifications will say something like this: "Hey, this post is trending, and based on the hashtag, you might want to respond as your company." You can respond as your company and get involved in conversations to bring attention to what your company does. It's a great way to raise your company's brand awareness.

Featured Groups

If your company has created a group, you'll be able to associate them with your page.

The Admin Menu & Admin Tools

The **Admin** menu is at the top of your company page and allows you to monitor your page and keep it updated. The menu consists of content, analytics, and activity.

Content

To keep your page relevant, you need to post content. Content is what will drive people to your page. **[Strategy #37]** LinkedIn knows creating content takes time and effort, and many people struggle with producing it regularly, so they have made it easy for you to align your content to your audience via content suggestions. You can filter and find trending articles to share on your company page in the **Content Suggestions** area. You can filter available content using the following criteria.

- All LinkedIn Members
- Page Followers

- Employees
- Topics
- Industry
- Location
- Job Function
- Seniority

Once you've set your filters, you can share valuable information and articles with your followers directly to your company page with a couple of clicks.

Analytics

Your company page analytics are broken into three areas: visitors, updates, and followers. Under the **Visitors** tab, you can see various visitor metrics and even who follows your page.

Visitor Highlights

The **Visitor Highlights** section provides a quick snapshot of page visits over the last thirty days. The snapshot includes the number of page views, unique visits, and the number of times someone clicked your button.

Visitor Metrics

Visitor metrics visualize the visitor highlights in a graph and defaults to the last thirty days; but you select different ranges to view as well. You can also look at visits to specific pages within your company page, such as your Home, About, People, and Insights pages to see how your page is performing with unique visitors. By default, the metrics you see are for desktop views only. You can aggregate both mobile and desktop views by toggling on the little switch on the right-hand side.

Visitor Demographics

Visitor demographics allow you to view visits to your page, but you can also break those visits down by visitor type. In this section, you can view your visitors by the following criteria:

- Job function
- Location
- Seniority
- Industry
- Company size

Reviewing this information will give you an idea of the types of people visiting your page, so you can see if your messaging is attracting the right audience.

Activity

The final item in the Admin menu area allows you to view activity on your page to see who is interacting with your content so you can respond promptly. Notifications you'll find here include the following:

- Reactions
- Shares
- Comments
- Mentions

Understanding who is interacting with your content can help you build new connections and relationships. When someone mentions your company, you get notified and can respond directly to the person who mentioned you. Likewise, if someone comments on your post, you can quickly respond. The **Activity** area is a great way for you to see the individuals interacting with your content. Some may follow your company, some may not, but each interaction is an opportunity for your company to shine.

Admin Tools

The **Admin Tools** dropdown menu on the right-hand side allows you to manage various aspects of your company page. For example, you can invite your personal profile connections to follow your page. You can sponsor post updates (paid ads), you can post a job, create an event, and create a showcase page (more on this in a minute). From the Admin area, you can also set admins for the page, edit the page URL, or deactivate your page. These tools require a little more attention: creating a showcase page and creating an event.

Showcase Pages

Showcase pages are a unique way for your company to highlight products and services.

To create one, you click the menu item under the Admin Tools area, then follow the same steps to build your company page. With a **Showcase** page, you get an About section, where you can talk specifics about your product or service. You can post text, images, documents, and videos to your showcase page like you can with your company page.

Events

LinkedIn recently added this feature for companies to post events they are hosting. Creating an event can be an excellent way for you to expand your reach to folks outside of your current sphere of influence. To create an event, you click on the menu item and complete the pop-up window details. Once created, your event will appear on the right-hand side of the feed on your main page.

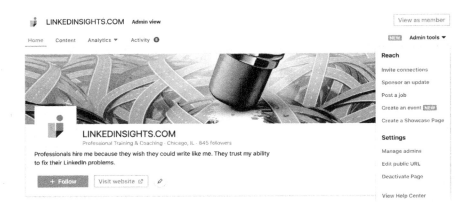

LinkedIn Events allow you to create and join events of interest to you. Events can be meetups, online workshops, seminars, and where you hold webinars for your products or services. Events allow for enhanced opportunities for you to join communities, grow your network, and even learn new skills. Once you've created an event, both organizers and attendees can issue invites (if the event is public) to promote your event. There are two types of roles for **Events**; organizers and attendees.

The Organizer

The *Organizer* is the event's host. This person can create events, invite attendees, and even include additional participants. The *Organizer* can be either an individual profile or a LinkedIn page.

The Attendee

The *Attendee* is a LinkedIn member who accepted an invitation to attend an event. Attendees can participate in discussions with other attendees and post content in the Event feed.

Once created, events can't change, but you can manage the details at any time. When you update the details of your event, the attendees are notified. Organizers and attendees can access a list of participants and start interacting via messaging or inviting them to connect before the event.

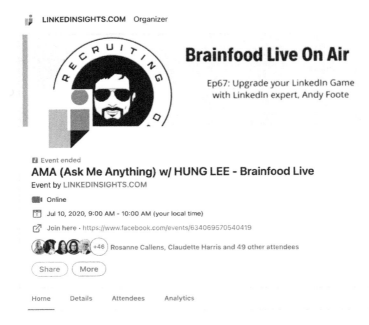

LINKEDINSIGHTS.COM   Organizer

Brainfood Live On Air

Ep67: Upgrade your LinkedIn Game
with LinkedIn expert, Andy Foote

🎞 Event ended

AMA (Ask Me Anything) w/ HUNG LEE - Brainfood Live

Event by LINKEDINSIGHTS.COM

📷 Online

📅 Jul 10, 2020, 9:00 AM - 10:00 AM (your local time)

↗ Join here · https://www.facebook.com/events/634069570540419

+46 Rosanne Callens, Claudette Harris and 49 other attendees

(Share) (More)

Home   Details   Attendees   Analytics

Searching on LinkedIn

Prospecting on LinkedIn

Finding your audience on LinkedIn can feel like prospecting for gold. You dip your pan in the flowing river, scoop up rocks and silt, shake the pan, and see what falls out. In other words, for most people, finding the right connections feels like it requires a lot of luck—unless, of course, you understand how to search on the platform. You can perform three types of LinkedIn searches: Basic, Advanced, and Sales Navigator.

Basic Search

 Q Search

Basic search is at the top of your profile in the menu area. To use it, you simply type in your search criteria and hit Enter. LinkedIn will return a variety of possibilities from people to companies to groups and even jobs. It's a mishmash of options. You can do better. Using the magnifying glass icon in the search box's right-hand side provides you with a more structured searching method where you can search by people, jobs, content, companies, schools, or groups.

People Searches

Searching for people is exactly what it sounds like; you search for someone by name. To open the **People** Search, select *People* from the search menu, put the name of the person you are searching for in the box, and hit Enter. LinkedIn will show you a list of people with the name you entered.

Use the people search when looking for someone specific, maybe someone you met at a networking or LinkedIn event. To help narrow your search, LinkedIn provides you with the following filters:

- Connections: 1st or 2nd level
- Locations: City, State, Country
- Current Companies

You can use one filter or all three. Filters will help you find your "person" quicker than just typing a name in the search box.

Job Search

As you would imagine, LinkedIn is well positioned for job searching and candidates can do a lot of research on potential openings without leaving LinkedIn. Job search offers the most filters within the basic search. The following are some of the parameters you can use to find your ideal position.

Sort By:

- Most Relevant
- Most Recent

Date Posted:

- Past 24 hours
- Past Week
- Past Month
- Any Time

LinkedIn Features:

- Easy Apply
- Under 10 Applicants
- In Your Network
- Fair Chance Employer: These are jobs posted by employers who have signed pledges to hire people with criminal records.

Company:

Search for current opening by company

Experience Level:

- Internship
- Entry Level
- Associate
- Mid-Senior Level
- Director
- Executive

You can also search by clicking All Filters to find a few additional criteria.

- Salary Range
- Industry
- Job Function
- Title

- Commute = Remote
- Benefits

Once you have selected all of your filters, you are presented with a list of job openings. You can apply within LinkedIn by sharing your profile, but in many cases, you will be redirected to the company's website to provide additional information. If a job opening has the *Easy Apply* button enabled, you simply click the button, then LinkedIn pulls all of your data from your profile and sends it directly to the company. No resume required.

Content Search

Finding relevant content on LinkedIn is easier than you might think with the **Content Search** feature. You can do this using one of two methods: the hashtag or content search parameters.

Hashtag Search

[Strategy # 38] A hashtag search is when you type a keyword into the search box with a hashtag in front of the word. For example, #freelancing will show you posts using the tag "freelancing." The hashtag search is an excellent way to sort your news feed, so you only see content related to the hashtag you are interested in seeing. Hashtags are becoming very relevant on LinkedIn. Check out the detailed section on hashtags later in the book.

Content Filters

Like the previous search method and those yet to be discussed, you can use filters in the content area to quickly narrow your focus. The filters include the following.

Posted by:

- Me (You)
- 1st Connections

Date Posted:

- Past 24 hours
- Past Week
- Past Month

Author Industries

Opens a search box for you to type in an industry.

You can select **All Filters** as well to find one additional criterion. We don't know why it's not in the menu, but you can also search by author companies when you click the All Filters button.

Company Search

There are no filters for companies. You type in a company name, and LinkedIn pulls it up, assuming the company has a company page.

School Search

Just like with a company page, you can search for schools as well. There are no filters here either. Simply type in the school's name, and if they have a page on LinkedIn, it will show up.

Group Searches

Groups can be a great place to find people in your area of expertise or interest. If someone is in a group, they are most likely there because they are interested in the group topic. To find your group, type in your keyword or area of interest to find groups relevant to the term. You can then visit the groups and join the ones you feel are most appropriate.

Advanced Search - Boolean Search

We're going a bit "ninja" here, but you can significantly enhance your basic searches using Boolean Operators. Boolean Operators allow you to narrow your search by combining keywords with modifiers. **[Strategy #39]** A Boolean search helps you get more relevant results by limiting your search to defined parameters. We'll walk through an example shortly, but first, let's review the specific Boolean Operators (modifiers) you can use during a LinkedIn search.

Boolean Operators

There are four types of operators you can use to construct your searches and narrow your results.

Quoted Search

A **Quoted** Search allows you to look for an exact phrase when you enclose your keyword in quotation marks. Quoted searches are great when searching for a multi-word title. Here's an example of a Quoted search:

"product manager" or "program manager" or "LinkedIn trainer"

When you use quotes, LinkedIn only provides the exact phrase between the quotation marks. You will get a list of product managers, program managers, or LinkedIn trainers in this example. Without the quotes, your list will be a list of people who use the words product, program, LinkedIn, trainer, or manager in their profiles.

NOT Search

NOT (all capital letters) is an exclusion search. The term NOT is used directly before a keyword search term you want to exclude from your search. Here's an example of a NOT search:

"product manager" NOT "program manager"

This search will present you with profiles containing the term product manager and exclude the term program manager. NOT searches are great when you want to limit the profiles to a specific certification or title.

AND Search

The opposite of a NOT search is the **AND** search. An AND (all capital letters) search is inclusive. The results you get will include all the items in your search criteria. Here's an example of an AND search:

"product manager" AND "program manager"

As you can imagine, the AND search will show you any profiles containing the keywords product manager and program manager. These searches are great if you are looking for someone with multiple specific skills or titles.

OR Search

The **OR** (all capital letters) search broadens your searches to include more than one item in your keywords. Here's an example of an OR search:

"product manager" OR "program manager" OR "marketing"

The OR search is useful if you are looking for a broader profile pool to review. Usually, this type of search is conducted when looking for multiple certifications, skills, or titles.

Complex Search

Technically referred to as a parenthetical search (but who says something like that), combining Boolean search terms allows you to do more complex searches to get you closer to the exact results you seek. Here's an example of a parenthetical or complex search.

"president" NOT (VP OR assistant)

A note on searching for titles. Many job titles are generic, meaning you can apply them in many different ways. For example, if you type *president* in the search box without using Boolean, here are some typical results:

- President
- Vice-president
- Vice-president in charge of sales
- President of sales
- President of operations
- Vice-president of marketing
- Administrative assistant to the president
- Administrative assistant to the vice-president of operations

The list goes on and on. As you can see, this is not particularly helpful when narrowing your audience, and will impact your campaign effectiveness. Use Boolean search terms to help you focus on the profiles most important to your campaign, whether you're looking for a new role or new clients. Boolean will improve your results.

*Note: Boolean works in the keyword fields on LinkedIn.com and works in the company, title, and keyword fields in **Sales Navigator**.*

Search Limitations

You can do a lot with a basic search, but you will see your results increase when using Boolean. However, LinkedIn limits the amount of searching you can do by imposing what it refers to as commercial search limits. LinkedIn does not define a specific number of searches you can do each month. However, there is a limit, and when you get close to this mysterious number, LinkedIn will send you a message stating you are close to the commercial limits.

LinkedIn knows its business users are heavy searchers. Businesses use LinkedIn every day looking for prospects for new business or candidates for open positions. On the flip side, regular users (you and I) only use the search function occasionally. When you approach the commercial limit, LinkedIn is kind enough to give you a warning. If you hit the limit, LinkedIn will stop you from searching until your monthly usage resets on the first of the month.

You can read more about commercial search limits here – https://www.linkedin.com/help/linkedin/answer/5295.

Sales Navigator

LinkedIn's solution to avoiding its commercial search limits is to upgrade your account. LinkedIn has several advanced tiers to help gain more search power, but we're only going to discuss **Sales Navigator** (SN) for this book.

Should You Upgrade to Sales Navigator?

This question comes up often. Here's the truth you don't want to hear: it depends. It depends on how and how much you use LinkedIn. Here are some criteria for you to consider, presented in no specific order.

- Do you regularly hit the commercial limits?
- Are you searching for prospects on LinkedIn?
- Are you using LinkedIn to generate leads for your business?
- Would you consider yourself a heavy searcher?
- Are you looking to narrow your search results?

If you answer yes to these questions, then you might want to consider upgrading. If you answered yes to the commercial limit's question and it prevents you from meeting your sales quota, you might want to upgrade. At the time of publishing, Sales Navigator runs $79.99 a month for a single seat.

For the majority of you reading this, upgrading to SN is probably not necessary. But if you use LinkedIn regularly to find leads and prospects, it might be worth upgrading because there are a lot of really cool things you can do with Sales Navigator.

NOTE: It may help your decision process to know that while SN can help you find your ideal audience quickly, it's messy. At the time of publication, everything you do in SN is contained within SN. You can't export a list easily to your CRM, for example. You can do it via third-party software, but third-party software is frowned upon by LinkedIn.

Sales Navigator Features

Sales Navigator is a premium product within LinkedIn. It is separate from your regular LinkedIn interface and has a different look and feel. SN is designed to give you timely information about your ideal audience.

Your Feed

The feed in SN is very different from the feed in "regular" LinkedIn. For starters, there are no advertisements or sponsored posts cluttering up your feed. The feed in SN is designed for one purpose: to help you engage with your ideal audience.

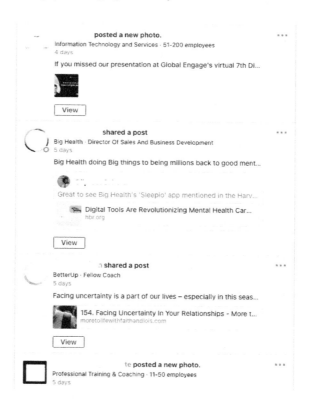

Advanced Filters

The most significant advantage of upgrading to SN is the advanced search filters. The advanced filters allow you to slice and dice your searches in many different ways. One of the first things you'll do in SN is set up the search criteria for your ideal audience. Once created, LinkedIn will use this criterion to search for your ideal audience continuously. Here are a few of the search parameters you can use in combination within Sales Navigator:

- Keywords
- Past leads and accounts
- Geography
- Relationships
- Language
- First name
- Last name
- Seniority level
- Years in position
- Years at a company
- Function
- Title
- Years of experience

Filters for Companies

- How many people work at a company?
- Company
- Headcount
- Company type

Other Filters

- When somebody became a member

I don't know why this search is necessary. If you know of a good use case for this search, send us an email to let us know.

- Groups
- Schools
- Tags

Bonus – You can also use Boolean searches within companies, titles, and keyword filters. As you can imagine, these filters can be very powerful in finding only the LinkedIn profiles that interest you the most.

[Strategy # 39] Tagging Feature

If you're using LinkedIn to find prospects and generate leads, the ability to tag people using SN may appeal to you.

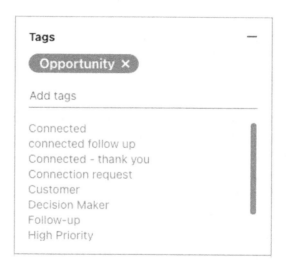

A tag is simply a label you apply to a lead within SN. Tags help you track the status of people in your "sales funnel." For example, a Sales Navigator funnel might use the following tags.

Tag 1 – Connect Request Sent
Tag 2 – Connected
Tag 3 – Thank You Note Sent
Tag 4 – Conversation

Tag 5 – Offline Request

Every time you move a prospect down your funnel, you simply check the next tag in your list. We go into greater detail about how to do this in the next chapter.

NOTE: Creating a sales funnel on LinkedIn is a very manual process. LinkedIn's goal is to have the entire experience "feel" like you are at a networking event and making a genuine connection. While more work for you, it's one of the ways LinkedIn is different from other platforms.

Lists

There are two types of lists you can create in Sales Navigator: lead lists and account lists. Lead lists are for individual members, and account lists are for companies.

Account Lists

[Strategy #40] Account lists are great for keeping tabs on a specific company. If you are a sales rep, for example, account lists help you track when your current customers or desired ones post something or are mentioned in the news. When this happens, you get notified in your SN feed. The notification allows you to respond and stay engaged in a timely manner, so you stay or start to become top of mind to your prospect company.

Lead Lists

Lead lists contain a list of individuals in your ideal audience. Using the search parameters noted above, you can create a lead list for a specific audience. Once your lead list is set up, LinkedIn will notify you anytime someone who fits your search criteria is identified. Like an account list, anytime an individual on one of your lists likes, comments, shares, or posts something on LinkedIn, you get notified in your feed so you can respond accordingly.

Once you've set up your lists, SN breaks your list up into the following categories for you.

895	48	535	138	3
total results	Changed jobs in past 90 days	Posted on LinkedIn in past 30 days	Share experiences with you	Leads that follow your company on LinkedIn

Total results

Exactly what it sounds like, the number of people who meet your selected search criteria.

Changed jobs in the last 90 days

Since most people update their profiles shortly after taking a new role, LinkedIn knows who has moved into a new position. Knowing who switched jobs recently allows you to reach out and congratulate one of your audience members.

Posted on LinkedIn in the last 30 days

One of the biggest challenges with finding prospects (leads) on LinkedIn is knowing whether someone is active. As you might guess, many people create profiles then forget to log back in or forget the platform altogether. As a regular user, you have no way of knowing who is active and who is not. With SN, you do. This particular category is something automated bots can't see, so when you use them, there is a percentage of prospects who will never see your message—another reason not to use bots.

Share experiences with you.

This breakout provides you with a way to reach out to potential prospects by letting you know who belongs to the same groups you do. You can use this information in an introductory email since it's something you have in common, or you can use it to determine which of your groups contain your ideal audience.

Follow your company

This breakout is not as significant as it used to be since LinkedIn started sharing this information on your company page. However, it is nice to know who follows your company page, and since SN is separate from regular LinkedIn, having this information here prevents you from needing to jump back and forth between the two systems. Oh, one thing to note here. If your personal profile shows you work for two different companies, SN will not tell you which specific company your prospects are following, only that they are following one of them.

Viewing Profiles

When viewing profiles on SN, LinkedIn displays some additional information at the top. For example, here's how SN shows Andy's profile:

As you can see, there is a quick high-level snapshot of Andy so I can quickly glean pertinent information. All of his contact information is on the right-hand side, which is why we stressed the importance of completing this information in the profile chapter. Just below his contact information, SN allows me to create notes on Andy, which could include things like interactions or the status of your connect request.

Other things you can quickly see are where Andy works today, previously, and where he received his education. Additionally, you can determine how many contacts you have in common and even review his recent activity on LinkedIn. LinkedIn also provides a suggestion for the best way to get an introduction to Andy through your network.

There is a lot more to Sales Navigator than what we've covered here—in fact, entire books have been written on it. We hope what we've shared gives you the necessary information to decide whether or not it might work for you or your organization.

Links and Profiles Mentioned

LINKS

- Commercial search limits – https://www.linkedin.com/help/linkedin/answer/5295

PROFILES

- Gina Riley - https://www.linkedin.com/in/ginariley/

PART 3
Convert

Message Prospects

Messaging on LinkedIn

Messaging on LinkedIn is daunting. Maybe it's because we're so used to getting spammy, automated messages from people (bots), we're concerned about coming across the same way to others. Two common messaging questions are:

1. What do I say?
2. How do I respond?

We'll answer both in this chapter.

Networking

As we've mentioned a few times throughout this book, LinkedIn is a networking platform. Nowhere else is that more apparent on the platform than in messaging. As much as it can, LinkedIn wants networking on the platform to mimic real life, which means they want connection requests and messaging to be genuine, which of course, poses a challenge for businesses who want to connect with people for selling.

More than anything, LinkedIn wants you to use the messaging feature to build rapport with people, which is challenging to do at scale, hence all of the messaging bots and spammy messages. If you view messaging on LinkedIn as an opportunity to build rapport, you'll quickly understand why trying to sell something in your first message will turn people off. It's no different from meeting someone for the first time, handing them a business card, and going right into your sales pitch; it doesn't work. Instead, it would be best to make your communications (messages) match how you interact with someone in person.

The LMS Messaging Funnel

[Strategy #41] The LMS Messaging Funnel provides you with a consistent and personable method for your messaging interactions. The funnel will help you answer these questions:

1. What do I say?
2. How do I respond?

Here are a few ground rules before you begin using The LMS Messaging Funnel.

The LMS Messaging Funnel is a manual process.

LinkedIn wants your interactions to be personal. When implementing your funnel, keep in mind it is meant to be manual, meaning you'll respond to every interaction yourself. This does not mean you can't use pre-written templates or scripts, but it does mean **you** (or someone who works for you) should enter the templates into the messaging box yourself. At the end of this chapter, we'll share a tool you can use to make your interactions more "automated."

Do not automate this process.

When we say automated in this context, we mean third-party applications, typically using a Chrome browser extension. Because messaging is challenging to do at scale, it's tempting to automate this process and let the bots run free. Think twice before you do. Numerous companies will help you automate your interactions on LinkedIn, but before you spend a dime on them, keep in mind **automation is against LinkedIn's policies**, and they actively seek out automated behaviors. Using automation is a quick way to get put into "LinkedIn jail" or banned altogether. Should this happen, it is tough to get out and there is no get-out-of-jail-free card.

LinkedIn Messaging Pitfalls

Before we dive into the LMS Messaging Funnel, we want to point out a few messaging pitfalls on LinkedIn.

Not Researching

[Strategy #42] Before you respond to someone on LinkedIn or send a connection request, take a few minutes (or even just one minute) and review the person's profile. Look for something you share in common. If you're struggling with this, **[Strategy #43]** scroll to the Interests section at the bottom of their profile. Once you know what you have in common, mention it in your message. Another great place to research is the recent activity section of someone's profile to find a nugget to mention.

Selling

Your goal on LinkedIn should not be to sell. Your goal should be to make genuine connections and build rapport. Selling is an offline activity. Instead of selling, build a relationship, and see where things go naturally.

Not Being Human

Simple rule: If you wouldn't say it in person, don't say it in messaging. Imagine yourself standing in line to get tickets to a movie. Would you tap the person in front of you on the shoulder and deliver your sales pitch? Of course not. So don't do it on LinkedIn either.

Not Asking Questions

Those who want to sell, pitch. Those who want to build relationships ask questions. **[Strategy #44]** When messaging on LinkedIn, your goal should be to get a response. A great way to do this is by asking genuine questions. Questions form the foundation of a good conversation and can quickly lead to building rapport and trust. Questions also keep a conversation going.

The Phases of the LMS Messaging Funnel

The LMS Messaging Funnel consists of three phases: (re)connect, converse, and convert.

Phase #1 - (RE)CONNECT

Your goal in this first phase is to get your audience to accept your connection request or to reconnect with an old connection. That's it. **[Strategy #45]** Do not use LinkedIn's default messaging. Take the time to research your prospect. Go to the person's profile and find commonalities to mention in your message. Here are a few examples of messaging for connection requests. These examples are guidelines for your messages, not absolutes. They need to be tailored and personalized for your ideal audience.

Connect #1

Hi [NAME],

I came across your profile and noticed you're in [INSERT INDUSTRY]. I love [INSERT AN AREA OF INTEREST OR COMMONALITY]. I'd like to connect and keep track of what's happening in the space.

Your Name

Connect #2

Hi [NAME],

I reviewed your profile and noticed we are in a similar space/industry, and I thought I would reach out to connect.

Your Name

Connect #3

Hi [NAME],

I noticed we are both members of the [INSERT NAME OF GROUP], and I'm looking to connect with fellow group members.

Your Name

Connect # 4

Hi [NAME],

I was searching for [INSERT TOPIC] when I noticed your name. I reviewed your profile and noticed we have a similar interest in [INSERT INTEREST], so I thought I would reach out to connect.

Your Name

Connect # 5

Hi [NAME],

I was searching for companies in the [INSERT INDUSTRY] and your profile stood out. It looks like you've done some pretty cool things, such as [INSERT COOL THING], so I thought I would reach out to connect.

Your Name

Reconnect – Use when reaching out to someone you are connected to but have not spoken with yet.

"Hey [NAME],

I was reviewing my connections the other day, and I realized we've never had a conversation about {INSERT TOPIC}. I was wondering if you're still involved with [INSERT SOMETHING FROM PROFILE]?

Your Name

Phase #2 - CONVERSE

The goal of this phase, Converse, is to start a conversation. You are not selling. Instead, you are building rapport and, hopefully, a relationship with your connection. The Converse phase of the funnel consists of two smaller steps: cheers and contribute.

Step 1 – Cheers

The goal of your Cheers response is twofold. First, it's to thank them for becoming a connection. Second, it's to start a conversation. **[Strategy #46]** After someone has accepted your connection request, respond within a day or two at most. Don't let weeks go by without responding. Think of this message as you would meeting someone in public. Waiting too long to respond to questions or introductions makes things awkward.

Right after an accepted connection request, **[Strategy #47]** send a thank you note. The note does not need to be fancy, only an acknowledgment of your new connection. **[Strategy #48]** Use the Cheers message to start a conversation by asking a question. The question you ask needs to be relevant to your connection, so do your research. Here are some examples of possible Cheers messaging.

Cheers Message #1

Hi [NAME],

Hi, thanks for connecting. I am curious, [INSERT A QUESTION]?

Your name

Cheers Message # 2

Hi [NAME],

Thanks for connecting! I hope you don't mind, but I took a look at your [WEBSITE/LINKEDIN PROFILE/ COMPANY PAGE]. I loved your post [INSERT NAME OF POST]. I'm curious about your thoughts on [POST SUBJECT/RELATED INFORMATION]?

Your name

Cheers Message # 3

Hi [NAME],

Thanks for connecting. I enjoyed [SOMETHING FROM THEIR PROFILE, OR A RECENT POST OR ARTICLE]. [ASK A QUESTION ABOUT THEIR PROFILE, OR SOMETHING THEY POSTED].

Your name

Step 2 – Contribute

Great! You've asked a question and initiated a conversation. Now your goal is to continue the conversation to build rapport and trust. Your goal in this stage is to contribute or start adding value to your new connection. Once we've started a conversation, **[Strategy #49],** you'll provide your connection with relevant content or information to help them professionally. The information you provide can be content you created, or curated content. Whichever direction you choose, the content needs to be relevant enough to add value. Like all messages previously, personalize these messages as well. Here are a few examples.

Contribute # 1

Hi [NAME],

I hope you're doing well this week. When I was [POSITION/ TITLE], I struggled with [INSERT PROBLEM]. Have you ever experienced that? Anyway, I found/created this [RELEVANT CONTENT] that helped me overcome [THE PROBLEM], which led to [INSERT SUCCESS].

If you'd like a copy of [RELEVANT CONTENT], let me know, and I'll send it over.

Have a great day.

Your name

Contribute # 2

Hi [NAME],

I found this article you might find interesting. It's a simple list/guide about [NAME of PROBLEM], but it got me thinking about it differently. Anyway, here's the [INSERT LINK]. Hopefully, you find this as useful as I did. Have a great day.

Your name

Contribute # 3

Hi [NAME],

Did you see it? The [INSERT ASSOCIATION NAME] recently published an article about [INSERT PROBLEM], and I thought it might be useful for you. You can read the article at [INSERT LINK].

Have a great day.

Your name

Contribute # 4 - LinkedIn Event or LIVE (can also be used in the Convert phase)

Hi [NAME],

I wanted to let you know I'm holding a LinkedIn Event (LIVE) about [INSERT PROBLEM] and how to overcome it. If you're interested, here's where you can sign up [INSERT LINK].

Your name

The key to Contribute is to provide value and ask questions so you get responses. **[Strategy #50]** When providing a piece of valuable content, it's always better to ask for permission to send it versus just sending it. Otherwise, you're like the people in Vegas handing you flyers to some show you have no desire to see. If they say yes, send them a simple reply.

Contribute: Prospect says YES –

Hi [NAME],

No problem. Here it is. If you have any questions as you review it, let me know. Happy to help.

Your name

[Strategy #51] If your connection says no or they ignore you, wait a couple of weeks before re-engaging them. If they say no or ignore you a second time, you should assume they are not interested, and leave them alone.

Contribute: Prospect says NO –

No worries [NAME]. Have a great day.

Your name

Phase #3 - CONVERT

Nice work! You've built up a rapport and possibly some trust by providing your connection with some valuable and relevant content. Your goal in this phase is to continue building rapport to move your connection to an offline conversation. The offline conversation is still not a sales pitch, but it may become one. Your offline conversation can take many forms.

- A webinar
- A phone call
- A Zoom call
- A LinkedIn event

- A LinkedIn live
- An in-person event (if they are local)

[Strategy #52] Whatever the format, your goal in this phase is to take the conversation offline. Here are a few examples of messaging you can use to ask people to engage with you in an offline discussion.

Convert #1 - Webinar, Event, or Live Invite

Hi [NAME],

I wanted to let you know I'm hosting a [WEBINAR/ LINKEDIN EVENT/TRAINING] specifically for [AUDIENCE] on [INSERT DATE].

During the [WEBINAR/LINKEDIN EVENT/TRAIN-ING], I will talk about how to overcome [OBSTACLE].

Would you be interested in attending?

You name

Convert #2 - Phone or Zoom Call Invite

HEY [NAME],

I was working with a client recently on [PROBLEM/ OBSTACLE]. I think the solution we developed may be valuable to you if you're looking to achieve [SUCCESS].

If you're up to it, I'd love to jump on a quick call and share what we were able to achieve. I think the solution could be something valuable to you as well.

If you're interested, let me know when a good time for a short call would be. (Alternatively, you can name a day and time frame for them to select).

Your name

Convert #3 - In-person Event

HEY [NAME],

I was working with a client recently on [OBSTACLE]. I think the solution we developed may be valuable to you.

If you're interested, let's jump on a quick call. Would [INSERT TIME AND DATE] be a good time to chat?

Your name

Even with all these messaging script examples, you may not get your connection to the Convert phase, and that's okay. If at some point it feels natural to have an offline conversation, you will, but don't force it.

Key Points to Remember When Messaging on LinkedIn

1. **[Strategy #53]** Start conversations.

2. Don't try to close a deal on LinkedIn. Your goal is to take the relationship outside of LinkedIn, where you can have more relevant conversations.

3. Always research prospects before sending or responding to messages.

4. **[Strategy #54]** Personalization is key to social selling. Like in real life, you will resonate with some clients and not others. Be yourself and let the conversations lead to a natural "selling" point.

5. **[Strategy #55]** Ask questions. Questions form the foundation of a good conversation and can quickly build rapport and trust.

6. Keep the conversation going. It may take six or more messages to get to where your connection is comfortable with an offline meeting.

Bonus – Gorgias Templates

Using third-party software to automate anything on LinkedIn is against the user agreement, and you run the real risk of being banned or suspended if you break this rule. However, you can safely "automate" your messages using **[Strategy #56]** a Chrome extension called Gorgias Templates. (https://www.gorgiastemplates.com/)

Gorgias Templates (GT) was developed to help you write emails quicker, but you can use it with any messaging application. GT is a Chrome browser extension, but it does not connect with or scrape data from LinkedIn, like other third-party extensions, so it is safe to use. With Gorgias templates installed in your browser, you can **[Strategy #57]** create pre-written messages to use in the message box with just a couple of clicks. Imagine having all of the templates above loaded into GT, and with the click of a button, you have a script in the messaging box you can quickly personalize before clicking send.

[Strategy #58] You can use GT to create your LMS messaging funnel. For example, you could have messages for all of the following.

- Profile View
- Followed Me
- Post View
- Connect
- Converse – Cheers
- Converse – Contribute
- Convert – Webinar
- Convert – Phone call
- Convert – Zoom
- Convert Event – Live, LI Event, In-person.
- Campaigns – Like Ryan's *CareerKred* book giveaway

The options are limitless. To make the most of GT, prepopulate 80% of your message and personalize the remaining 20%. This feature alone will save you time by not typing every response individually.

Bonus – Email

Email is still one of the best methods for converting your audience. **[Strategy #59]**. Put the LMS Messaging Funnel to work in email. Here's how that would work. Once you've found your ideal prospects, visit their profiles and find their email address. If they do not have an email address listed, find someone else in their company using the company page with their email address listed. Since all emails in a company are structured the same way, once you have one email address from a company, you essentially have every email address at that company.

[Strategy #60] If you can't figure out their email address, you can use a third-party app like Hunter.io to find the email address for you. You can also review posted articles, the About section, or their current Experience section on their profile for email addresses. If this sounds "sneaky" to you, keep this in mind, you are only contacting people in the way they want you to contact them. Meaning, they added their email address to their profile so people would contact them. **[Strategy #61]** The same is true for phone numbers. If they list their phone number as a contact method, it's okay to call them.

Post Content

"What should I post on LinkedIn?" We hear this question a lot, but before we provide an answer, there's another question you should ask first: "Why should I post content on LinkedIn?"

Why Post Content on LinkedIn?

The simple answer is that content reinforces your positioning and messaging while helping you build credibility and trust with your ideal audience. If that's not enough, here are three more reasons you should post on LinkedIn.

Awareness

Your content helps build awareness for your brand. Specifically, who you are, what you are all about, how you add value, and most importantly, how others benefit from your services.

Thought Leadership

Thought leadership is one of those "buzzwords" that gets batted around a lot. Simply put, thought leadership is you demonstrating your expertise through content. Thought leadership adds to your credibility by showing others your level and depth of knowledge on a particular topic, subject matter, or area of expertise. Thought leadership positions you in someone's mind and makes it easier for them to think of you when they hear someone mention your area of expertise.

Fit (Culture)

If you're a business owner or job seeker, pay attention to this one. **[Strategy #62]** Creating content helps others determine what it would be like to work with you. If you want to get hired, either as an employee (business of one) or a contractor, the content you post helps others determine if they can work with you or if you would be a good fit to work with their team on a project. **[Strategy #63]** Take time to review and clean up your social media and online presence. Even if your content is top-notch, one wrong post or tweet can sabotage your perceived fit.

What to Post on LinkedIn?

Now that you understand why you should post on LinkedIn, let's get to the "what" question, specifically, what type of content should you post? The simple answer is to post content your audience will be interested in reading. The point of posting content is to demonstrate your expertise, which means you don't want to post content for the sake of posting content. To ensure your content aligns with your brand and demonstrates your expertise, consider using high-level themes and topics aligned with the themes.

Themes

[Strategy #64] Content themes will help you maintain a consistent message. Without a theme, it's easy to "go off the rails."

Selecting a theme helps you narrow your focus, so you stay in your lane. When selecting a theme, start with a problem you solve.

Topics

[Strategy #65] Topics fall under a theme; they are the subject of your content, and they should highlight your expertise. Topics are the individual stories you share to highlight your skills, thought leadership, and engage your audience. Topics can include the following:

- Something you've learned
- Something you've taught
- A problem you've solved
- Customer conversations
- Something you agree or disagree with within your area of expertise
- A subject relevant to your audience

While not an exhaustive list, topics can be about anything as long as they fall under your theme. Sarah Johnston, the Briefcase Coach, is excellent at turning her personal life stories into relevant topics for her audience while staying in her career coaching and resume writing theme. Once you have your themes and topics, the next step is to create content. For this part, we recommend using the content pyramid.

The Content Pyramid

[Strategy #66] The content pyramid is a visual representation of the types of content you can post on LinkedIn. The pyramid consists of four types of content: written, images, audio, and video.

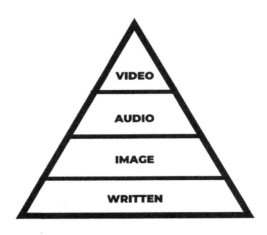

Written

Written content is the foundation for the pyramid and is used for posts or articles.

Images

Images can be graphical, quotes, infographics, or even pictures of you at an event. They are great for posts and articles.

Audio

Audio files can be used in articles and posts. An audio file can be as simple as you reading one of your posts or a snippet of your podcast.

Video

You can upload videos to your feed, LinkedIn Stories, and if approved, you can do LinkedIn Live. **[Strategy #67]** Upload your videos directly to LinkedIn rather than having a third-party tool like Buffer or Hootsuite do it for you. LinkedIn's algorithm prefers uploaded video.

Repurpose Your Content

Now that you know what to post on LinkedIn, it's time to talk about getting the most from your content on the platform. Most people get so hung up on posting something new they forget about the content they've already published. After publishing a piece of content, ask yourself how else can share or reuse your content. **[Strategy #68]** People consume things differently, so when considering repurposing your content, reference the content pyramid to help you understand the other types of content you can publish. For example, if you start at the bottom of the pyramid (written) and work your way up, you could take your post and create an image. Maybe an image quote from your post? You could also turn your published post into an audio file by recording yourself reading it. Finally, you could flip on your phone's camera and record yourself reading your published post, and now you have a video.

When to Post on LinkedIn

Another important aspect of posting content on LinkedIn is cadence. Cadence is when you will post stuff to the platform. Most people think of cadence as a time and date, but cadence is more than a time and day to publish. Cadence is really about consistency and frequency. **[Strategy #69]** Your cadence is your cadence. It will be different from ours and anyone else who is reading this book. Don't let other people's cadence influence your posting rhythm/schedule. Decide when you want to post and build a routine. Are some times better than others to post? Perhaps, but we'd prefer you focus on being consistent rather than selecting a particular time.

[Strategy #70] Once you've chosen your cadence, identify your themes and create a list of topics to discuss. With your theme and topics in hand, assign a theme to a month and schedule your topics each week. If your cadence is weekly on Tuesdays, for example, then assign a topic to every Tuesday in the month. If your cadence is every other week, then assign a topic every other week. The great thing about cadence is you decide not only when to post but also how often.

Using Hashtags

While hashtags may feel "new," they were used on LinkedIn as early as 2010. After a three-year experiment, LinkedIn retired hashtags (initially referred to as Signal), apparently because not enough people used them, which makes sense because non-influencers (i.e., you and me) couldn't write articles or posts until 2014. Additionally, no content algorithm regulated content distribution, and followers weren't a thing.

If you haven't noticed, LinkedIn—as with so many other new features like native video, live video, reactions, and most recently **Stories**—tends to play catch-up and prefers to take its cues from other social channels. So, it's no surprise LinkedIn reintroduced hashtags in 2018. Unfortunately, they provided virtually no guidance or best practices on how to use them properly.

As a result, LinkedIn users assumed the more, the merrier, and all of a sudden, posts were filled with a hashtag soup like you see on Instagram, which immediately feels very spammy to most users. Thankfully Pete Davies, former Senior Director of Product Management, stepped in and advised users on the proper use of hashtags. Pete said three hashtags were the magic number. But things change all the time on LinkedIn, and the sweet spot is now between three and nine hashtags.

How to Use Hashtags on LinkedIn

[Strategy #71] Pete also suggested hashtags can help your post get a higher ranking (algorithm – more on that a little later) in someone's feed depending on the hashtags they follow. "If a connection uses a hashtag you also happen to follow, your post gets an extra boost." While that sounds all well and good, it begs the question, how do you know if someone follows the same hashtag? Truthfully, you don't. If you knew who they were, you could ask them, but that's not possible currently. Besides, asking everyone what hashtags they follow sounds like something an engagement pod (more on that in the next chapter) would do.

Popular Hashtags vs. Branded (custom)

Should you use your own custom hashtags, like #CareerKred, #AndyDoesLinkedIn, #LinkedinMadeSimple, or use the popular ones followed by many people? Unfortunately, reviewing *Follower* counts and how often hashtags appear in LinkedIn search results, doesn't tell us much. Believe us, Andy has tried, but no one seems to have a conclusive answer to this question, and if LinkedIn knows, they're not sharing this information with users.

Adding to this confusion, LinkedIn makes it incredibly difficult to determine which hashtags have the most followers. You have to conduct search, after search, after search. It's painful, almost as if LinkedIn doesn't want you to have this data. Maybe it's because they don't want us to focus on the most followed hashtags. After all, they saw what happened to **Groups** years ago when they ranked them by size.

The truth is, when it comes to branded versus popular hashtags, we may never know what LinkedIn prefers. **[Strategy #72]** Our advice is to use one hashtag for your brand and the other two to eight for popular ones relevant to your audience and content.

Trending Hashtags – Don't Get Too Excited

If you have been posting and using hashtags on LinkedIn, then you've seen this notification: "Congrats, your post has been trending in #xxxxx." Don't get too excited; this is a "phantom notification." Why do we call it a phantom notification? Because when you click on the = *View hashtag* button, you are taken to a curated hashtag feed that shows your post right there at the top. So, it certainly does seem like it's trending, right? Try refreshing the URL, and boom! You are no longer at the top of the curated feed. Why LinkedIn sends out this notification, we have no one idea, and it isn't apparent. Maybe LinkedIn is sending us the notification just to get us to click it? If so, you have no idea if your posts are doing well or just doing.

The Future of Hashtags

Overall, we think hashtags will become a critical part of your LinkedIn experience in a few years. I mean, wouldn't it be amazing if we knew which hashtags were being searched for, used, or clicked on the most? How cool would it be if you knew which country, city, or person used which hashtags? While we don't have that data yet, Andy firmly believes we'll get LinkedIn hashtags V.2, where LinkedIn will share all kinds of juicy data with users (maybe just the premium paying users). Think of Google Analytics for LinkedIn hashtags, and remember where you heard this first, folks. In the meantime, stick to three to nine hashtags in your posts.

Links and Profiles Mentioned

PROFILES

- Sarah Johnston – https://www.linkedin.com/in/sarahdjohnston/
- Pete Davies – https://www.linkedin.com/in/petejadavies/

Content Vehicles

Posting on LinkedIn

Once you have your content and you know your cadence, you need to start posting. In LinkedIn, there are three places where you can publish content: your profile feed, company page feed, and articles.

Your Profile Feed

Your feed is what you see when you log into LinkedIn. It's right there in the center of the screen on a desktop and the only thing you see on mobile. You have one feed for your personal profile and one for your company page. The feed is where you interact with others, create posts or articles, upload videos or other content you may want to share. The feed is where you demonstrate your thought leadership and raise your brand awareness. **[Strategy #73]** A key component of your daily activities on LinkedIn is to like, comment, and share other people's stuff right in the feed. Let's take a closer look at what you can do in your feed.

Posts

A post is a short-form piece of content. Posts can be updates or well-thought-out pieces of content you publish. Posts help you demonstrate your expertise and help you become known for knowing something. To post something to your feed, click in the post-module at the top of your feed in the area that reads *Start a post*.

LinkedIn allows you to use up to 1,300 characters for your posts, which includes your hashtags. You can add videos, images, and documents to your posts as well. When in the post-module, LinkedIn allows you to choose who can view your post. You can select from the following choices:

- Anyone – Anyone on or off LinkedIn.
- Anyone + Twitter – Same as above, but you also post to Twitter.
- Connections Only – Only those connected to you will see your post.
- Group Members – Only members of groups you belong to will see your post.
- Advanced Settings – Turn off commenting on your post.

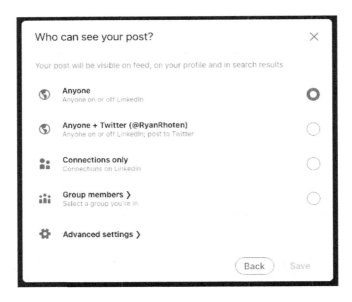

Once selected, click *POST*, and your content will appear in your feed.

Types of Posts

In addition to plain text posts, you can create other types of posts as well.

Video Post

On a desktop, you upload your video directly, and on a mobile device, you can create a video post on the spot.

Document Post

A document post could be anything from a white paper to a slide show. You upload your document directly, and LinkedIn will display it as a scrolling document, commonly referred to as a carousel. **[Strategy #74]** Carousel posts are highly effective at capturing the attention of LinkedIn's algorithm from a Dwell Time standpoint. More on this later.

Articles

Articles are long-form content. Think long blog posts. Articles can contain up to 110,000 characters. You can add images, videos, slides, links, and even snippets to your articles. Articles are great for building your thought leadership.

Polls

Ever wonder how your audience feels about a particular topic or question? **[Strategy #75]** Posting a poll might be a great way to get direct feedback from your audience. Polls originally existed on LinkedIn in Groups. They disappeared for a few years, but they are now available for individual users and group admins.

You can create polls both on the mobile app and desktop. Questions are limited to 140 characters. You can add up to four voting options, with each answer limited to 30 characters. You can set the poll duration to last from one to three days or one to two weeks. Completed polls can be found in a search. Poll authors can select who gets to see the poll and some basic stats.

Celebrate an Occasion

Have a new teammate or launching a project? LinkedIn provides a way for you to celebrate those occasions and more as a post.

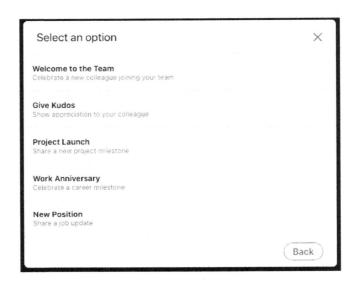

Find an Expert

If you need some expert advice or assistance, LinkedIn has a quick way for you to find help with the *Find an Expert* post. When selected, this post will ask for some basic information such as the category you need help with (think marketing, coaching), where you are located, and a brief description of the assistance you need.

Add a Profile

If you've ever wanted to highlight someone—an employee or a supervisor, for example—the *Add a Profile* post allows you to add someone's profile to a post quickly to acknowledge them for a great accomplishment.

Share That You're Hiring

Want to get the word out about a new role in your company? With the *Share That You're Hiring* post, you can very quickly create a post letting those in your network know you're hiring!

Offer Help

If you have specific expertise or you just want to help others out, the *Offer Help* post is a quick way for you to let others know you're willing to help them out. Once you've selected how you want to help, LinkedIn prepopulates a post starting with the hashtag for the area you're offering to help.

Feed Engagement

In addition to creating content for your audience to engage with, the feed is the place for you to engage with your ideal audience's content. There are three main ways for you to engage with other people's content: Likes (reactions), Share, and Comment.

Likes (Reactions)

Likes used to just be...likes. Today they are more commonly called reactions, and LinkedIn has really "spiced up" how you can react to someone's post. At the time of publishing, there are six ways you can react to someone's post:

Like   Celebrate   Support   Love   Insightful   Curious

Like
Support
Celebrate
Love
Insightful
Curious

[Strategy #76] Don't just be a "Liker." If you react to a post, it's good practice to share in the comments why you reacted the way you did.

Comments

Too many people react to posts without leaving comments. Maybe they're strapped for time; perhaps they're concerned about what others might think; whatever the reason, we look at it as being lazy. **[Strategy #77]** Comments are where the "magic" happens on LinkedIn. It's where you meet new people. It's where you share your insights and information. It's a critical factor in staying visible and becoming known for knowing something. So, don't cop out anymore. Get in your feed and leave some legitimate comments and insights.

Commenting tip: Engage in a real conversation, not a drive-by. When commenting, avoid one-word responses—"Great!"—as they come across as inauthentic. **[Strategy #78]** Instead, share your experience/point of view, and be courteous. "That's a great point @Steve, what's your opinion on X? I understand it has become more popular recently?" or "Curious to know more about this. Do you have any sources or pointers @Phil?" Maybe, "I agree 100% @John. I was thinking the same thing."

Jane Jackson Career Coach ICF · 1st   1w ···
Career Coach ✳ LinkedIn Top Voice 2020 ✳ Author of #1 bestseller N...

Excellent round up A N D Y F O O T E – am enjoying CH so far - can
see that it could potentially take up a lot of time! Interesting
conversations and I'm testing it out with Wendy Pavey this afternoon
at 5pm Sydney time to see how it goes for #jobseekers - so far I
notice that it's predominantly for entrepreneurs, small business
owners and creative professionals. What are your thoughts? Oh, by
the way I'm @janecareercoach (following you already!) #clubhouse

Celebrate · 2   Reply · 4 Replies

A N D Y F O O T E Author   1w ···
Reassuringly expensive LinkedIn brand enhancer

I just followed you (back)! Definitely a time suck but it
depends on how you're measuring ROI and whether you're
trying to leverage other networks (i.e LinkedIn). I'm finding a
ton of people are closing the loop from CH to here, which is
smart. I think there's scope for building presence/audience
and adding value, regardless of your professional objectives.

I predict employers using CH to spot talent and interview job-
seekers quickly and efficiently, for example 'pitch to our panel'
and if we select you, let's continue the conversation in a
private room. Job fair + Screener + Interview + Salary
negotiation in a day. Let's speed this up 😜

Like · 🖐 2   Reply

Wendy Pavey · 2nd   1w ···
Executive Brand Strategist ◆ Advising leaders how to create ...

A N D Y F O O T E That's a fascinating prediction and with
your permission, Jane and I will share it in our upcoming
Clubhouse room. It would be wonderful to hear a hiring
manager talk about their culture and corporate goals, so an
interested person could get a better idea if the company
would be a good fit. That could save so much wasted energy
applying for the wrong roles.

Like · 🖐 2   Reply

A N D Y F O O T E Author   1w ···
Reassuringly expensive LinkedIn brand enhancer

Wendy Pavey absolutely, feel free.

Like · 🖐 1   Reply

Jane Jackson Career Coach ICF · 1st   1w ···
Career Coach ✳ LinkedIn Top Voice 2020 ✳ Author of #1 best...

A N D Y F O O T E brilliant suggestion - and I'll enjoy joining in
your rooms on #Clubhouse too.

Support · 🙋 1   Reply

Suggested Comments

Another recently added feature in your feed regarding posts is the *Suggested Comments*.

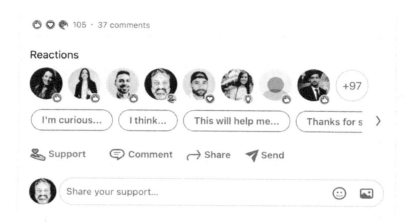

As we've mentioned, LinkedIn loves engagement, even if it needs to "fake it." At the same time, suggested posts may be great for saving some time and, in many cases, may be close to what you'd write anyway. **[Strategy #79]** We recommend only using them in messaging, not in comments. Responding to posts with actual comments is how you start conversations and meet new people. Little speech bubbles aren't going to cut it. But for those of you who typically do quick drive-bys ("Awesome!", "Love it!", "You rock!"), suggested comments will be "Perfect!" Just know they won't help you get more views, leads, or build stronger relationships.

Engagement Pods

As people look to increase their views on LinkedIn, they looked for ways to "engage" the algorithm, and the **Engagement Pod** was born. An engagement pod is a group of people who all agree to engage with each other's content, usually within the first hour of posting. The idea behind the pod is the more engagement a post gets, the better the chances are of having a more extensive audience see the post.

Engagement pods happen in the messaging section of LinkedIn or any other outside communication channel. Each engagement pod has different rules, but essentially the gist of them all is when someone in the pod publishes a post, they put a link to the post in the pod, everyone is notified, and agree to collectively "engage" with the post. There are two concerns you should consider before starting or engaging in a pod.

First, pods are inauthentic. You're getting engagement not because your content is excellent or thought-provoking, but because people agreed to engage with it. Second, and maybe more importantly, you will be engaging with content that may or may not be relevant to your audience. When you like or comment on something, a percentage of your network is notified. If they review what you engaged in and find it not relevant, they will become less likely to engage with the content you want them to see.

Now that you know what they are and what they do, we'll leave the decision of whether pods are good or bad for your brand up to you. If you'd like to learn more about pods, here are two comprehensive articles:

"The Pros and Cons of LinkedIn Engagement Pods" by Matthew Dooley – https://www.linkedin.com/pulse/pros-cons-linkedin-engagement-pods-matthew-dooley

"Your Guide to LinkedIn Engagement Pods" by Josh Steimle – https://www.joshsteimle.com/linkedin/linkedin-engagement-pods.html

Groups

While not quite what they used to be, Groups are still a great place to connect with other professionals who share common interests. **[Strategy #80]** Here is the key to getting the most from LinkedIn Groups: join groups where your target audience hangs out.

You can join up to 100 groups, so take time to identify the right ones for you. As you now know, you can search for groups by typing in the search bar then selecting Groups as your main criteria. Once you've found a few groups where your audience hangs out, say five to seven, click the *join group* button, and be patient as some groups may be slow to approve your membership.

Once admitted, read the group rules, then introduce yourself and start adding value by engaging with other group members in discussions. **[Strategy #81]** Always remember to be helpful. No selling in the group! Even though you can send unlimited messages to other group members, this does not give you a license to spam everyone in the group. Don't be that person. Everyone hates unsolicited, "salesy" and uninformed messages. Take time to build a relationship, get to know your network, and work to understand their needs/pain points before you even think about pitching or writing that offer to help.

Dan Roth, LinkedIn's Editor-in-Chief, recently said a team is working on Groups and that LinkedIn had made "an investment," which users will see play out sometime this year (2021). The fact that LinkedIn continues to work at improving groups and Dan's hint of forthcoming changes is why we're still bullish on the future of groups on LinkedIn. Create and join them, don't ignore them, position yourself to fully leverage them because they will become more useful over time.

LinkedIn Stories

LinkedIn is following Snapchat, Instagram, and Facebook by introducing LinkedIn Stories. You can use Stories on company pages where you are the admin and on your personal profile. Stories let you share images and video up to twenty seconds in length, and like the other platforms, your Stories are only available for twenty-four hours. **[Strategy #82]** Stories provides LinkedIn users with another way to go to the market.

Fun fact: LinkedIn initially launched Stories in Brazil. Why Brazil? According to LinkedIn, Brazil is the third-largest video content producer on LinkedIn because Brazilians have a worldwide reputation for creativity.

Stories do not appear in your feed and, at the time of publishing, are only available on the mobile app where they appear at the top of your **Home** feed as a circle. Click on the circle, usually the *story* creator's headshot, or the company logo if an organization has created the *story*, and the image or video will be displayed. You can "splice" a longer video into several *stories*, but your viewers will see a short gap every twenty seconds. To pause the *story* while viewing, touch the screen with your finger, then lift it to resume playing. The "X" at the top of the story allows you to leave Stories at any time.

[Strategy #83] When creating a *story*, we recommend using the vertical camera angle versus the landscape view. The vertical image provides the best size (9:16) aspect ratio. Because approximately 80% of videos on social sites are watched in silence, add subtitles to your *stories*. As a producer, you can add stickers/text to your story and tag (@mention) people. As a viewer, you get to watch, and you can message the producer as long as you are a first- or second-degree connection. Sorry, third degrees. **[Strategy #84]** Don't forget to brand your Stories by adding your logo or a custom hashtag. If you want to see Stories done right, follow Cher Jones. She is absolutely amazing.

LinkedIn Live

LinkedIn Live (LL) is another way to connect/shine on the LinkedIn platform - if you're lucky enough to be selected. At the time of publishing, LinkedIn Live is still in "beta" and requires approval from LinkedIn to gain access. If you're interested in applying, here's the link – https://www.linkedin.com/help/linkedin/ask/lv-app.

LinkedIn Live is a live video streaming feature that allows members to broadcast videos with their network in real-time. **[Strategy #85]** If approved, technically, you can "go live" whenever you want to, but the best *Lives* require significant planning. If you want to see a fantastic *Live* show, tune into Cher Jones's weekly #JustAskCher Live show. You'll quickly get a feel for the amount of planning that goes into producing a live show.

We've watched several LinkedIn Lives, and at this point, many of the streams have been hit-and-miss, just not must-watch-live content. However, we do commend folks for getting their message out there. It takes courage to go live, but courage needs to be mixed with proper planning to produce a watchable show. Just because you can "go live" doesn't mean you should.

As mentioned previously, LinkedIn **Live** is still in beta and is still pretty unfinished and a little quirky. It's kind of like riding a feisty showjumping horse for the first time, blindfolded in an arena with a handful of rotating audience members. At this point, LinkedIn can't host thousands of live streams at once and will need to tightly control the quality of content, or who knows what could show up in your feed.

LinkedIn Live Approval Process

The following are the selection criteria LinkedIn reviews before approving you to use LinkedIn Live. LinkedIn provides no insights into which of the items below hold more weight regarding approval, so we suggest treating them all as equal.

- Video and overall content creation history*
- Audience size and engagement history
- Member or Page account has been in good standing

- Two Factor Authentication (2FA) enabled in account settings

* We believe having a large body of video work is possibly the major factor in getting approved for LinkedIn Live.

LinkedIn Live Rules

Once approved, it should come as no surprise that there are rules, best practices for you to follow when you go live, such as:

- No selling or promotional streams.
- No pre-recorded content. All streams should be live and happening in real-time, or you may confuse members and potentially betray their trust.
- No live streams shorter than 10 to 15 minutes because there won't be enough time for the audience to increase and interact. You can share shorter videos from your homepage.
- No meta streams. Avoid talking about how to use LinkedIn on LinkedIn.
- Avoid sponsor logos that dominate the video. If you must use sponsor graphics, keep them small.
- No lengthy "starting soon" screens. Don't keep your audience waiting for more than one or two minutes.
- No unprofessional streams. All live content is publicly visible and should be appropriate for a LinkedIn audience.

Last thing to note on LinkedIn Live: If you get access, you'll need to sign up for a live streaming software provider. LinkedIn provides the platform, but you need to provide the means. There are at least twelve (and counting) live stream platforms you can use, each requiring its own degree of technical ability to learn, and most (except for Stream Yard) come with a monthly or annual fee to use.

LinkedIn Newsletters

Newsletters are new; you may not have even heard of them yet. Essentially, they are a subscribe button for your articles. At the time of publishing, **Newsletters** have been in beta for over fifteen months and are gradually rolling out to all LinkedIn users. LinkedIn is purposely rolling out newsletters very slowly because they want to avoid notification overload. **[Strategy #86]** When you get access to the Newsletter feature, you'll be able to invite your first-degree connections to subscribe. After subscribing, they'll be notified every time you publish an article on LinkedIn. At least, that's the theory. Newsletters appear to have been warmly received by many content creators on LinkedIn. The Newsletters feature is an exciting move on LinkedIn's part and is perhaps a recognition that all content that keeps users on the platform is good.

Links and Profiles Mentioned

LINKS

- "The Pros and Cons of LinkedIn Engagement Pods" by Matthew Dooley – https://www.linkedin.com/pulse/pros-cons-linkedin-engagement-pods-matthew-dooley
- "Your Guide to LinkedIn Engagement Pods" by Josh Steimle – https://www.joshsteimle.com/linkedin/linkedin-engagement-pods.html
- LinkedIn Live application – https://www.linkedin.com/help/linkedin/ask/lv-app

PROFILES

- Matthew Dooley – https://www.linkedin.com/in/matthewrdooley/
- Josh Steimle – https://www.joshsteimle.com/linkedin/linkedin-engagement-pods.html
- Cher Jones – https://www.linkedin.com/in/itscherjones

BONUS –
The LinkedIn Algorithm

Okay. We know you probably skimmed everything else in this book and jumped right to this chapter looking for the mother of all strategies—"gaming the algorithm." So, we want to be crystal clear on this point: This chapter intends to inform and educate you on how we believe the algorithm works at the time of publishing. Not to teach you how to "game the system."

Since the algorithm is the single biggest thing impacting your content success on LinkedIn, we wouldn't be doing our job if we didn't include a paragraph about the algorithm in this book. Andy spends a lot of his time on LinkedIn experimenting and collaborating with other LinkedIn experts like Richard van der Blom, trying to discern how the algorithm works. We believe if you're going to play the game, you should know the rules.

The LinkedIn algorithm governs reach on LinkedIn and changes regularly. Please follow Andy as he posts his findings and other experts' conclusions in his LinkedIn feed and on his website if you are interested in understanding the latest updates and assumptions. At the time of publishing, here are three significant changes resulting from our inaction related to the algorithm.

The 1% Are Stealing the Limelight

LinkedIn doesn't talk about the algorithm much, but it is usually notable when they do. In a post found on the LinkedIn Engineering Blog titled, "Spreading the Love in the LinkedIn Feed with Creator-Side Optimization," LinkedIn announced they had adjusted the algorithm to generate more engagement on the average user's posts while counteracting "irrelevant hyper-viral posts (which) were gaming the feed and crowding out posts from closer connections."

This change came after LinkedIn realized users were not posting as many updates (posts) because the previous version of the algorithm relied mostly on content from top creators. In other words, users were writing less because they couldn't get in front of their audience and hated that the 1% were getting most of the eyeballs. A LinkedIn spokesperson said at the time, "Members like seeing more content from people they know." Really? No shit, Sherlock.

[Strategy #87] The algorithm shares more of your content with your connections instead of relying on content from influencers whom you may or may not care about or follow. Additionally, the algorithm now watches for "bad behaviors" designed to game the feed (engagement pods?).

Dwell Time

The second most significant algorithm tweak in recent times is something called **Dwell Time**. LinkedIn data scientists knew they needed a better mousetrap—clicks and "Viral Actions" think reactions/re-shares/comments, were not giving them enough of a "steer"—when determining which posts should get more attention. So, they got creative and decided to measure something else, which became much better at signaling real user interest: Dwell Time. **[Strategy #88]** With the rollout of Dwell Time, the algorithm began to measure when we slow our scroll on the feed, when we hover, and how long before we bounce away from the content.

Andy likes to say, "Our dwell is our tell." Meaning, what we pause on, we are interested in reading. This algorithm tweak improved the relevance of content each user sees in their feed. While engagement is still the ultimate objective, time spent browsing the post is measured now, which informs the algorithm of the type of content you like so it can serve up more of the same.

Dwell Time also plays a significant role for LinkedIn when it comes to monetizing your feed. The feed is the place where advertisers pay to promote their services and products, and it is prime real estate seen by millions of users every day. When users decide to spend less of their precious time sifting through content in their feed, LinkedIn stands to lose boatloads of cash. If you think about it, Dwell Time is a win-win.

What the Dwell?

Even in our ever-increasing digital world, words matter. Maybe more than ever before.

Realizing that Dwell Time is an impact metric for the algorithm, people started looking for ways to find an advantage, so they started writing "baity" first-liners to grab your attention. Once they had your attention, they tried to influence the Dwell Time metric by creating lots of white space in their posts.

Meaning, once they capture your attention with a catchy headline:

They write a single line of text, then hit Enter,
for every sentence.
Thus, "dragging" you through the post,

while at the same time increasing the
dwell time for their post, which increases the chances
of the algorithm catching on and showing their post
to more people.

See the point?

Andy refers to this as "broetry." While we believe in making your posts both readable and scannable, this technique is a pretty obvious one to game the algorithm. Fortunately, while the algorithm determines who sees your post, if you don't provide value, if there's no meat in the sandwich, the dwell bot will take notes, and you'll have fewer readers next time you post. **[Strategy # 89]** So don't be a Dwell-hole. Write and share content your audience wants to see, not content for the sake of the algorithm.

Long Tail Engagement

Have you noticed? Your posts now attract attention and engagement over days, not just hours. The "Golden Hour" is no longer a thing. The average shelf life of a post is three to five days. **[Strategy #90]** You still need to engage, but you don't have to baby the post within the first hours of publication. Relax. Engage at will.

While we're not 100% certain, this algorithm tweak may have been designed to "kill" engagement pods. Extending a post's shelf life to three to five days will make it harder for pods to coordinate their engagement, especially since most pod admins tell their members to engage within the "Golden Hour." I'm pretty sure no one is going to want to go back into the pod, find "older" posts, and engage with them a second time. This Long Tail change means authors can bank on a longer window to engage with their audience. You can publish and go about your regular business, come back to the post, and respond to comments at your leisure, rather than feel compelled to babysit the algorithm during what used to be the "Golden Hour."

Forget Me Not Penalty

If you decide to take a "longish" break from LinkedIn posting, the algorithm will mark you as absent. Yes, it keeps track of your cadence on the platform. When you return from your absence, you will find your post's reach will not be what it used to be. Additionally, your profile page views will plummet as well. **[Strategy #91]** We told you at the beginning of the book (you didn't skip that part, did you?) LinkedIn wants you on its platform, so it should make sense that your engagement decreases when you aren't.

How long is "longish"? It could be weeks, maybe months. Only LinkedIn knows for sure, and they aren't telling. We know that if you take an extended break from LinkedIn, your reach will be affected. So much so, it will feel like you are starting from scratch. And in a way, you are, because as far as the algorithm is concerned, you are only as good as your last post.

We know the algorithm assigns your content with a quality score before it is published. We believe every author has a score related to their activity, cadence, frequency, type, and effectiveness of content creation efforts. Additionally, LinkedIn measures how often you post, react, comment, respond and re-share. As we mentioned in the Content chapter (you read that one, right?), **[Strategy #92]** cadence plays an essential role in your content success on LinkedIn. So much so, LinkedIn talks about "posting cadence" when deciding whom to anoint as a *Top Voice*, as confirmed by Daniel Roth, LinkedIn's editor-in-chief.

"The first filter we use is quantitative: we look at engagement (including reactions, comments, and shares across each member's content), posting cadence, and follower growth."

Links and Profiles Mentioned

LINKS

- https://engineering.linkedin.com/blog/2018/10/linkedin-feed-with-creator-side-optimization

PROFILES

- Richard van de Blom – https://www.linkedin.com/in/richardvanderblom/
- Daniel Roth – https://www.linkedin.com/in/danielroth1/

BONUS –
Quick Reference Guide

Characters and Limits as of 2021

1. How many connections can I have? **30,000**
2. How many connection requests can I send? **3,000**
3. How many people can I block? **1,000**
4. How many groups can I join? **100**
5. How many groups can I start? **30**
6. How many companies can I follow? **As many as you want**
7. How many people can I follow? **As many as you want**
8. How much space in a connection request? **300 characters** (~50–60 words)
9. How much space in the About section? **2,600 characters** (~300–400 words)
10. How much space in the Headline? **120 characters** (~10–20 words)

30,000 Connections

Before you build your network, understand there is a cap, and once you reach that cap, you can't accept any more connection requests. **[Strategy #93]** So, connect for a reason. Don't connect for the sake of collecting people. Be strategic.

Connections automatically become followers. You can unfollow any one of your connections, but only one at a time. Last year LinkedIn allowed users to switch their connect button to follow (an option previously only offered to "influencers"). We've done this because we think it slows down connection request traffic, and we can direct this traffic by **[Strategy #94]** following a recent follower, which often results in the followed follower sending a connection request.

3,000 Connection Requests

[Strategy #95] Don't send a connection request to someone you want to connect with. Instead, follow them first, and maybe they'll send you one of their requests. If you need more connection requests, ask LinkedIn customer support nicely. If you've been in "LinkedIn connection jail" because too many people clicked, I don't know this person (*IDK*), you may not have your initial connection request quota increased. You can withdraw requests that have not been accepted. **[Strategy #96]** Withdrawing "stale" requests will replenish your balance of connection requests.

[Strategy #97] Be as specific as possible in your connection request. If you can't provide specifics of why you want to connect with X in your invitation to connect message, you are wasting everyone's time. Visiting X's profile before sending the request is an excellent idea.

You Can Block 1,000 People

When you block someone, they don't get a message and won't know unless they search on you and can't find your profile or content. You will be invisible and vice versa. The only time you will "see" the blocked person is when someone else tags them by name (and their name will be in black text, instead of tagged blue).

100 Groups

[Strategy #98] Treat LinkedIn Groups as databases. Make the most of your allowance. Why wouldn't you want to have access to potentially millions of people to whom you can send free group members to group member messages? LinkedIn recently dispensed with group member message limits (it used to be that you could only send fifteen messages per month). [Strategy #99] If you've got an excellent reason for building a group, do it. If there's a renaissance of LinkedIn groups, you'll be ready to capitalize. If not, you'll still have a little (or large) domain of your own.

Follow as Many Organizations as You Want

Job hunting? Follow your target companies. This won't necessarily get you the job, but it will show that you're doing your research.

Follow as Many People as You Want

Treat follow as a "nudge" or a "hello." Don't assume the algorithm will start sending you notifications after you've followed someone. You will need to engage in that person's content to signal to the algorithm you are indeed interested in that user.

2,600 Characters in Your About Section

The About section is your opportunity to tell your story and engage. Don't use third person, and don't bore or confuse the reader. Don't obsess about keywords (that's what the Skills section is for). Just focus on what you do, why you do it, and what you are doing now—or want to do next. **[Strategy #100]** If you use bullets, use • (and not weird/distracting symbols) for listing achievements, and support each accomplishment with facts, figures, stats, where possible.

220 Characters in Your Headline

You may see people with very long headlines and wonder how they got more characters than you. They achieved this by editing their Headline on the app until LinkedIn decided to offer the "extended headline" to desktop users.

Conclusion

Congratulations, you've reached the end! You now know more than probably 98% of all LinkedIn users based on what we've seen over the years. The question you have to answer now is, what will you do with this knowledge? How will you use it to make your business, career, and even LinkedIn itself better?

A Note on Shortcuts

The sooner people realize there are no shortcuts to succeeding on LinkedIn, the better. **[Strategy #101]** If some LinkedIn coach or guru tells you that doing X will help your posts get more reach, demand proof. Ask what their baseline performance is and ask to see the "technique" in action. For example, you may have heard about the "self-love" technique some LinkedIn gurus/coaches have been preaching. They tell you that liking your posts and comments will help you increase your reach, which is the kind of advice that gives LinkedIn coaches a bad name. There's no proof this "technique" will help with reach; in fact, it may harm it. Why? Because, as we've said before, LinkedIn hates any gaming/artificial boosting.

We think it looks desperate and is a bad look for the self-lover's brand and credibility. LinkedIn coaches or gurus who tell their clients to do this are selling snake oil. Do you actually believe you can get additional eyeballs on your content by liking your posts and comments? It's been suggested that the level of your social activity on the platform determines the perceived quality of your content. Really? Let's break that down. Some gurus have been espousing why your post went nowhere had something to do with your lack of engagement with other content.

Indeed, engaging with people who coalesce around your content shortly after publishing and regularly throughout the post lifecycle is solid advice. But being punished for not being an engager-in-general by somehow downgrading the "quality" of your content is genuinely bizarro, in our opinion. [Strategy #102] When it comes to LinkedIn advice, we recommend you follow your gut. If it sounds too good to be true, it probably is.

Our Final Dos and Don'ts

There's something about LinkedIn that forces people to look for quick fixes. Maybe it's because the potential is dangled in front of you by others, or perhaps it's because you don't want to do the work it takes to be successful on the platform. I'm curious...if you have children, would you ever tell them *not* to do the work required to be successful?

If you play the game right, there are significant benefits to be had on LinkedIn, but unfortunately, people want results fast, are impatient, or can't afford to wait. As a result, they engage in the following **DON'T** activities:

(1) Like their own content

(2) Use their company page to like their own content

(3) Like their own comments

(4) Mass-tag influencers

(5) Beg for engagement via messenger

(6) Use pods to boost content

(7) Hijack other posts and drop links

If you do any of these things, please stop. You're not doing your brand or reputation any good. If you want to ensure maximum success, raise your brand awareness and make sure your content is not read in silence. **DO** these things instead:

(1) Write amazing, unforgettable content which informs/ inspires/delights

(2) Create original content and experiment with different delivery methods

(3) Ask questions at the end of your post/article to get conversations started

(4) Build your tribe (audience)

[Strategy #103] Take the time to understand what your audience wants and give it to them every time you publish content.

[Strategy #104] Share what you know.

[Strategy #105] Show your personality.

[Strategy #106] Bring your A-game and win the "most liked comment" competition.

[Strategy #107] Remember: LinkedIn is a social networking platform, so it pays to use common sense.

This is how you win the LinkedIn long game. This is how you make LinkedIn simple.

LinkedIn Made Simple Program

(The "Pitch")

Rather than inundate you with sales information at the end of every chapter, as some books do, this is our only sales pitch for our companion (digital/online) program. We know many people struggle with LinkedIn. We also know this book will go a long way to show you how to leverage LinkedIn effectively. However, when it comes to actual implementation, additional online tutoring and one-to-one instruction are beneficial.

"I had no clue how to go about harnessing the power of LinkedIn. This course sorted that out! Clear instruction and outstanding step-by-step guidance mean that I'm now looking forward to conquering LinkedIn, rather than feeling confused and unsure." – Monica Sood, CEO Brand Clarity.

To help you go from "clueless" to conquering LinkedIn, we've developed a step-by-step program to guide you through everything we discuss in this book. The program is called LinkedIn Made Simple and can be found at LinkedInMadeSimple.com. The program includes:

- 50+ step-by-step videos
- Worksheets to help you complete every step
- Scripts and templates
- 3-month access to a private Facebook (FB) Group – If LinkedIn brings their Groups up to speed, we'll switch over to LI.

You will get access to the online videos and templates for as long as the course exists. Access will be limited to the FB group for three months for this simple reason: We want you to implement what you learn. The private FB group includes:

- Weekly Q&A sessions
- Direct access to Andy and Ryan
- Monthly training sessions
- Monthly profile reviews for members
- Interactions with like-minded members

We believe if you want to get the most from LinkedIn, there is no other program out there that can beat us. Are there cheaper ones? Sure, but you'll get what you pay for.

So, if you find yourself struggling with any of the steps in this book, visit LinkedInMadeSimple.com/Book, where you'll find a special discount only available to people who purchase this book.

Sales pitch over.

"This course took me from having no clue how to use LinkedIn to build my brand and generate leads to having a daily action plan for doing just that. Well worth the investment." – Pete Rakozy, Chief Growth Coach at SiteSmash.

"Excellent course if you want to up your LinkedIn game. I am totally clueless on the platform as I have never used it before, but LinkedIn Made Simple's hidden things will bring results in a way I never thought possible. If you need to understand LinkedIn better, this is the course for you." – Fabiana Beatriz Loverde de Huffaker, Personal Brand Photographer

Links and Profiles Mentioned

PROFILES

- Monica Sood – https://www.linkedin.com/in/monicasoodfahy/
- Pete Rakozy – https://www.linkedin.com/in/peterrakozy/
- Fabiana Beatriz Loverde de Huffaker – https://www.linkedin.com/in/fabiana-huffaker/

About the Authors

Ryan Rhoten

Ryan Rhoten founded CareerBrand to help brands—personal and business—eliminate the confusion and clutter distracting their customers from their core message, so they communicate their brand message in a simple and approachable way. Ryan excels at creating clear and concise brand messaging that cuts through today's digital noise, so you experience more impact, traction, and growth. In his first book, *CareerKred*, Ryan created a simple four-step process to build your brand online, so you get recognized for your expertise. In his latest book, *LinkedIn Made Simple*, Ryan and co-author Andy Foote create a very simple, easy-to-follow framework to help brands make the most of their LinkedIn experience. In addition to simplifying the complicated concepts of branding and marketing, Ryan is also a blogger, speaker, personal branding expert, and the host of the popular iTunes podcast, *The BRAND New You Show*, where he has interviewed over a hundred experts in the areas of branding and marketing.

Andy Foote

Andy Foote coaches individuals and organizations on how to capitalize on everything the LinkedIn platform has to offer. He's spent the last decade obsessively testing multiple engagement strategies while building a supportive and robust network on the most extensive professional networking website on the planet. He regularly shares his expertise and insights experientially via LinkedIn and his blog (www.linkedinsights.com). Andy has also recently launched his FOOTE-NOTES podcast, an interview show which seeks to shine a light on intrinsically interesting people, discussing their views on a wide range of topics, examining their career story, and figuring out what makes them "tick."

Made in the USA
Coppell, TX
27 May 2021

56303977R00095